Down To Earth

Down To Earth

The Spiritual Being's Guide
to a Happy, Human Experience

Glenn Ambrose

Down To Earth:
The Spiritual Being's Guide to a Happy, Human Experience

Copyright © 2019 by Glenn Ambrose

ISBN: 978-1-7330393-8-3
ISBN: 1-7330393-8-4
Library of Congress Control Number: 2019917209

Cover design and text by: Bear Marketing and Bill Van Nimwegen

Sacred Life Publishers™
SacredLife.com

Printed in the United States of America

Dedication

For my son, Matteo.
You were the Orb of Love that pulled me from
death's doorstep and began
this amazing journey.
I am forever grateful.

Contents

Acknowledgments

As I often do, I'd like to start out at the core which in all cases is The Divine Source. I thank the Loving Creator for the support and Love that's been expressed to me through experiences, synchronicities, and most importantly the expressions of its Self as the Beings I'm about to mention. Thank you for using me as the vessel to bring this book into the world.

I'd like to thank my son Matteo whose Love launched me into this spiritual life and has taught me what unconditional Love feels like on this earth. I'd also like to thank all of my family including my grandparents, parents, sister, brother-in-law, nieces, aunts, uncles and cousins. You all have played a part in the love that I've leaned on over the years. There have been some obvious times and some quiet times that are only known in my heart when your acceptance and Love has strengthened me and moved me forward. I needed each of these times to bring me to the place I am now and so I thank each of you.

I would also like to thank all the people who have been with me on this journey beginning with Douglas Muir who helped me open to a new way of Being. I was supported and guided through the early years with the help of many people in the fellowship of Alcoholics Anonymous as well as the 12 Step Program itself. To all my clients and my spiritual family in Rhode Island, you have supported me and helped me turn what was simply a hope to be of service into a reality. Without *all* of you, none of this would be possible.

With humility and deep thanks, I'd like to thank Peggy Johnson, my editor. You committed an amazing amount of energy and time to the creation of this book. The amount of shaping, wording, and grammar it takes to make a book a book is immense. You are a gigantic part of this project and I truly thank you from the bottom of my heart for bringing this to life with me! I'd also like to thank my publisher, Sharon Lund, who stuck with this first-time author as I navigated the ups and downs of the process while learning along the way.

Lastly I could not compile any list of thanks that didn't include the producers of my podcast *Life, Lessons, & Laughter with Glenn Ambrose.* Ben Barber and Dave DeAngelis are the engine that have propelled my message to the international audience it now has. The words "you should have your own podcast," has literally changed my life. I'd also like to specifically single out Ben Barber, to know him is to love him. Ben has been the single person there helping me every step of the way. He's been on every podcast, every business meeting, every idea, and stood by me supporting this message and me in general, year after year. This book is truly a culmination of our work together. Your help is heartfelt and greatly appreciated.

Introduction

Every journey is more successful with a guide. Climbing a mountain, going on a safari, or exploring a new place are all enhanced by a certain amount of knowledge. Avoiding pitfalls, knowing how to handle situations that you will encounter, and understanding which techniques are effective and which ones aren't can save you a lot of stress and confusion. We all have this knowledge deep within us however it's buried under years of social conditioning and domestication. For many of us, the ways we've learned to interact with life are flawed. These norms are so widely accepted by society, and therefore us, that we rarely slow down enough to realize how destructive they are.

We know that we can't buy happiness by acquiring material things. Then why, as a society, do we put so much energy into pursuing external goals and acquiring possessions? Even while knowing it's not the key to a fulfilling life, most people vigorously pursue this track. It's because we don't slow down enough to understand what these words truly mean. Even if we do, we certainly don't slow down enough to find an alternative path and then take an appropriate course of action. Perhaps in this fast-paced world, it's simply easier to keep moving along with the rest of the pack—the way we've been conditioned.

In this book, we're going to slow all the way down and hover there. We'll stand in the Truth and let it bubble up to the surface—even if it's uncomfortable seeing things we don't like and don't want to face. In so doing, we'll be more capable of seeing the reality of our dysfunction and be able to shift our non-effective ways of Being into healthier, more effective ways of Being.

My point is that we've been doing it backwards; we've been living from the *outside* in. We need to live from the *inside* out. Our happiness comes from within, which is then reflected back to us by our external circumstances. We need to slow down enough to recognize the Truth, see it for what it is, and then live from it. This book is filled with insights that can help you remember the Truth you already know deep within. It can help bring it up towards the surface and into your awareness. Once you begin to remember the Truth, you'll not only be able to recognize it, but also differentiate Truth from the misperceptions you've been living in. There is a knowingness at your core that you can feel. This is what you'll tap into in this book, the knowingness at your core which holds the Truth, the Way and the Path. When you see it you'll recognize it, as opposed to just intellectually understanding it.

For the first 35 years of my life, I rebelled. There was something inside me that knew the things I was being taught were wrong. Unconsciously I refused to let go of the Truth that was buried underneath all the conditioning. Being unconscious of what this Truth was, I suffered—dramatically. Eventually I experienced enough suffering to awaken—dramatically. After adjusting, learning the spiritual language necessary to express what I had opened to and interweaving my personal style, I began to teach. It was natural and comfortable. In learning to open and allow Divine Knowledge to steer the conversations with clients, during podcasts, blogs and vlogs, I've experienced a flow of information that I could not have come up with on my own. This Divine flow is insightful, intuitive, and always loving. It is beyond the capacity I have within myself alone and I feel joyful and humbled as it flows through me and out to help others. The following book was written in this Divine Flow with the mission to help and support people along their journey as Spiritual Beings having the happy human experience they desire and deserve.

My hope is that you will not simply read this book but slow down and absorb it. Being inundated with so much information in our society, it's easy to distract ourselves with gathering even more information in the hope of finding the key to happiness. We maneuver around pretending to grow while never Being who we want to Be. Read, internalize, and implement whichever sections connect with you most and then go back read, internalize, and implement the other sections afterwards if they connect with you later. This book is spiritual in nature so the connections you make with the teachings will vary with where you are on your path, constantly changing as you change.

There's a natural growth process to everything in a lifetime as well as over generations. There's a constant unfolding, opening, and expanding to become a fuller, more beautiful expression of oneself. We are at a point in history where we must open to a new way of Being based in Love to transcend the issues in our society once and for all. To embrace our new way of Being, we must learn to integrate our spiritual core with our human existence. This book provides clarity on spiritual law, how it works, and how to implement it in our everyday lives, giving us practical tools to enjoy our human experience to the fullest.

My wish is that this book will inspire you to shift your way of Being permanently, thereby improving your life and the lives of those around you. In turn others will awaken to new ways of Being through your example, producing the domino effect necessary for us to awaken as a species to the love, peace and joy we were meant to experience all along.

PART 1

SPIRITUAL FOUNDATION

Chapter 1

Spiritual Being Having a
Human Experience

Welcome. The title seems to have sparked your interest and you've decided to follow the nudge provided to you. You deserve a pat on the back and congratulations! You're already taking an important step in this journey: following the nudges. The words "a Spiritual Being having a human experience" resonated with you. They reminded you of something you already knew, something intuitively anchored inside of you as Truth with a capital "T," an eternal Truth.

As you contemplate the words in the title, pay attention to how you feel and where you feel it. You may notice that connecting with the Truth of these words is more of a bodily sensation than a mental exercise. You can feel the Truth in your body: often in your heart area, possibly in your stomach and torso, or even in your entire body. You may feel a comfort, a peace, a warmth, a tingling, or some sort of pleasurable sensation because you stumbled across a piece of Truth that your spiritual core has recognized and remembered. This is an important part of this book, as well as all spiritual texts, so pay attention to it. Allow yourself to slow down, feel it and become familiar with the feeling, so that you'll recognize it as you move through this book and your life.

This feeling is your guidance system, the guidance you've been seeking your whole life; the way to decipher what is True and right for you, and what is not right for you. If something in this book doesn't resonate with you, it simply means it's either not part of your journey or not part of your journey right now. It may come up again later and become part of your journey. If that's the case, it will

3

resonate with you. If it doesn't right now, simply dismiss it and move on. Paying attention to what resonates with you is an easy way to stay on your path and not veer off onto someone else's. Doing this is also a great way to attain wonderful information from multiple teachers without throwing away many valuable insights because you didn't connect with a few.

So, congrats on a part of you remembering that you're a Spiritual Being having a human experience! Remembering this is a huge step forward in the evolution of our species in general, as well as your own personal evolution. Now you can begin making sense of the rest of the core Truths that you remember and uncovering new things hidden beneath the conditioning of society's ways.

The beauty of this journey is that, as you walk it, you'll better see that the way you were conditioned and taught to live your life does not hold water. It literally makes no logical sense when dissected and looked at closely. Conversely, the spiritual Truth does hold water and makes logical sense in *all* ways, *all* the time, in *every* situation *always*. That's exciting stuff!

Gaining clarity about how the universe works in the macrocosm shows us how things work in the microcosm. It's the chaos theory in action. The farther we step back to gain a larger perspective, the clearer the Truth gets and the more things make sense.

What I show you in this book are the big-picture Truths and what they look like in our daily lives. We'll take a giant step back to gain perspective and then zoom into everyday life, using our new perspectives to make sense of our reality here on earth in a healthy, happy, productive, and fulfilling way. Sound like fun? It is!

So, let's start with the title: *The Spiritual Being's Guide to a Happy, Human Experience*. The Truth is that you are consciousness, awareness—a Spiritual Being. You are also here on earth to have a human experience. The journey we're on is to integrate these two aspects of ourselves. First to identify ourselves as Spiritual Beings at our core, to anchor ourselves in that and find safety in that—this is our foundation. From this foundation, we begin interacting with life on earth in a different, more playful, fun, and fulfilling way. We bring the safety of our eternal nature into the experiential reality of life, thereby enjoying our experiences as a temporary play with life. This is much more enjoyable than the all-encompassing and overwhelming attempt to achieve safety through the impossible task of controlling our external experiences.

The way to understand this is to look at our innate need for safety. Follow the logic with me. People want to feel safe. They long for it and desire it. If everyone has this need for safety, then it's innate. If it's innate, then it is divinely planned. The Creator created Beings with an innate desire to feel safe.

Most people try to achieve feeling safe through futile attempts to control situations and outcomes around them. This is not only frustrating, but it's impossible. It simply can't be done. Sometimes people succeed for short periods only to find that in the long term it doesn't work, which can be very confusing. If you achieve success at something and think it's because of you, you get attached to that success. You think you've "figured it out," which of course you haven't. The idea that you can control things is only temporary like everything else in this realm. If you're ever lucky enough to get your ducks in a row, someone comes by and kicks a duck out of line. Or one of those little guys wanders off after something—they *never* stay put.

Chapter 2

Temporal and Spiritual Realms

For the purposes of this book, I'll use the terms Temporal Realm and Spiritual Realm to distinguish between the two different realities we'll be discussing.

Spiritual Realm is the permanent state of reality where nothing ever changes; where what always has been will always be and where you will always exist. This is the realm and vibrational state of energy that never dies; it only transmutes into different forms while remaining itself. In the Spiritual Realm there is only Love, nothing else exists. There is no need to choose. All is well because you are loved completely, unconditionally, and eternally. Here the simplest of Truths lives, where everything, including us, is Love. The laws from the Spiritual Realm run the universe. They always have and they always will. They never change. What was True 10,000 years ago is True now and will be 10,000 years from now. This is why there is written record of sages speaking spiritual Truths thousands of years ago, and these same Truths apply today.

Temporal Realm is the temporary state we're in while incarnated in our bodies. Everything in this realm is temporary, constantly changing and in flux. Your car will be a pile of dust someday, new rivers will form; and your life situations will shift regularly and sporadically to give you different experiences through which to grow and enjoy your time here. This is the world of Yin and Yang, where every coin has two sides and where our perspective determines the reality in which we live, where we can experience either Love or fear. When "bad things" happen, you have a choice to open and grow from them, or to close yourself off and retreat from life. This is the land of free will where you have a choice over everything, including your perspectives, experiences, growth, resistance, suffering, and happiness. It's all up to you.

The concept of integrating these two realms can be explained by using movies and vacations as metaphors.

When you go to the movies, you can get somewhat involved in the movie. You go to experience something. So as you're sitting there your heart rate can increase: you can experience sadness enough to cry, you can get scared, and you can feel joy and even laugh aloud. However, a part of you feels safe from whatever is on-screen. When someone pulls out a gun, you don't dive under the seat or run out the door even though you would in "real life," because you know it's just a movie. You can be engaged and feel the emotions of the experiences, but not to the point where you get lost in them and think they're real.

At the movies you can get caught up in a story enough to feel different emotions, go on an adventure, and experience different things to some degree without completely losing your sense of safety. Even though your heart may jump at an exciting moment or you're brought to tears at a touching moment, you still know that it's just a movie. You can disconnect from the illusion of permanence shown on-screen. You can disconnect from the illusion of permanence in real life too. It's only temporary. That's why it's called the Temporal Realm.

This is how we're supposed to interact with life. We're supposed to let go of temporary illusion and anchor ourselves in the safety of the Spiritual Realm, knowing that we are eternal and loved and that all is well—always. From this seat of safety, we can interact with life in a similar way. We can have experiences, make decisions, and chase dreams without all the fear: the fear of failure; the fear of whether a decision is right; the fear of offending someone; the fear of not being good enough; and the fear of "what if?"

Knowing that we are pure Love, pure energy, eternal, safe, cared for, and unconditionally loved always is the foundation that grounds us. From this space, we can expand, grow, open, allow, remember our Truth, and experience different things without all the fear.

If we're anchored in the seat of spiritual safety, we can interact with life like we're on vacation. We know we'll be going home, and that this life is just temporary so we try new things and put less weight on our decisions. If we don't like something, we simply say, "I'm not doing that again" and then move on. If we like something, we might do it again if we have time. It's more laid back, fun, and enjoyable. It doesn't have all the pressure that ordinary life does. We need to interact with life in the same way. View it like a vacation or a game and be more playful. Our decisions don't matter that much. If we're moving toward what brings us joy, we're going to have a joyful life. If we don't, we won't.

If you go on a vacation and nothing is different, unexpected, or exciting, what's the point? You could just sit in your living room, save some money, and do nothing for a week. We go on vacation to experience different things. This is like our time here in the Temporal Realm. It's *supposed* to be different, ever changing, and exciting, just not in a way that causes so much stress and worry. Once we know that we are safe, that we are eternal, that we are energy—and that energy never dies but simply transmutes into another form—we can begin feeling the sense of safety we're supposed to feel and begin enjoying our fun, exciting vacation here in the Temporal Realm.

This is our journey. Too often, we focus on fighting or defeating something, such as our brain, our ego, our body's desires, our thoughts, our emotions, and so on. We must remember that we don't have to fight against anything. We have a mind, an ego, and a body for specific reasons. They are not our enemy. They are part of us and should be cherished for serving purposes that support our lives. Problems arise when we identify with them; when we think that this identification is who and what we are. We are not our minds; we are not our egos; we are not our bodies. We are Spiritual Beings, each walking around in a physical form that happens to have a mind, an ego, and a body.

The mind can solve problems and remind us of things we learned in the past to help us move forward. The ego is there to protect us from harm. It's always looking for possible danger, so that we can see it if it's there and protect ourselves from it. Our bodies give us the ability to experience this amazing world and the vacation we're on in countless ways through our senses. We are blessed to have each one of them. There is no reason to declare war on our support systems.

We can put more focus on the present moment and interacting with life rather than regretting the past or fearing the future. We can learn to understand that our ego is simply a warning system (which I'll go into more later) and not the be all and end all source of information. Just because our mind or our ego says something doesn't mean we have to believe it, take it as Truth, act on it, or judge ourselves for it. It's just a passing thought. We need to discern what we hang on to and what we let go of. There's a beautiful quote from *A Course in Miracles* (*ACIM*) that encompasses this Truth beautifully: "Nothing real can be threatened. Nothing unreal exists. Herein lies the peace of God."[1]

Your spiritual self cannot be threatened. It is eternal and shining as bright as ever. Nothing you've experienced has dimmed, dented, scratched, or damaged it in any way, shape, or form. You always have been and always will be Divine Perfection that is loved and safe at your core. This safety is your permanent, unshakable foundation.

Your physical body, your mind, and your ego can be threatened. They can be harmed, shaken, and hurt. Therefore, it is unreal. It doesn't truly exist. It's only temporary. If we know it's not "real," does it have to hurt? Only if we've identified with it. If I know my ego isn't real, but I feel wounded when someone says, "You're a bad person," I can simply recognize that it's my ego that has been hurt, not me. If I don't identify with my ego as being me, it doesn't hurt; or at the very least, I can work through it without developing resentment. It's just someone's comment about an imaginary thing that isn't me and isn't real. With the mind, dis-identifying works very similarly. As far as the body goes, it can certainly be more difficult to disregard physical sensations; however, for many advanced beings, this has been accomplished. For example, monks meditating in the mountains of Tibet in below-zero weather with wet blankets on them can raise their body heat enough to stay warm and dry the blankets. Amazing—and possible!

---

[1] https://acim.org/acim/what-it-says/

10

When we identify with the *ACIM* quote—that nothing real can be threatened and nothing unreal exists—we anchor in the Truth of what we are at our core and hold the temporary experience more loosely, herein lies the peace of God.

Chapter 3

Trying to Control an
Ever-Changing Reality

The reason people seek feeling safe is because we have an innate knowledge that we *should* feel safe. The issue is that we are seeking safety where it doesn't exist—in the Temporal Realm. This is why we tend to try to control things. We set things up in a certain way that gives us a false sense of security, and then we freak out when they don't go the way we think they should.

Most people have a habit of attempting to control things to some degree. This urge originates from the need to feel safe. If it seems like you can control something, it makes you feel safer. The problem with this is that you live in an ever-changing reality. With this system, there is no real safety because you can never truly control what happens in your life. You can never be healthy enough to never get sick, get hurt, or die. You can never love someone enough to protect him or her from everything. You can never be rich enough to never suffer, and so on.

The Truth is we *all* want to feel safe, yet safety is unattainable here on earth. So why would we all want something that's unattainable? The answer is that it *is* attainable. It's just not accessible where we're looking—here on earth. It *is* accessible in the Spiritual Realm. This realm never changes. It is eternal, and this is where our safety lies.

The spiritual journey that you are on is one of integrating your spiritual Truth with your human existence. You cannot abandon or deny either one if you hope to have integrity in who you are. You are a Spiritual Being having a human experience.

If you stand in the Truth of who you are as an eternal Spiritual Being—anchored in eternal Love *and* here on earth having a temporary, experiential journey—you will find the safety you seek. The safety doesn't lie in the Temporal Realm; it lies in the Spiritual Realm.

So, anchor yourself by connecting with whatever you believe in the universe: the Creator, the Divine, God, a higher power, or something greater than yourself. This needs to be your foundation, and from here you can feel safe while interacting with the uncertainties of life. Sit in the seat of God's safety; from there, you can play the game of life. From this vantage point, you won't take everything so seriously, nor should you. This is just a temporary vacation. You can't lose. You're destined to win because the entire universe is conspiring in your favor. Have fun, take chances, and live while you're here. Don't worry. The Truth of the matter is that at the end of it all, and even during it, you're safe.

Chapter 4

We Are Born Knowing the Truth

How and why did we end up struggling with our human experience if we already know the spiritual Truths at our core? Those are great questions. Do you want the good news first or the bad news? I'll start with the bad news and bring it home with the good news.

When we came into this world from the other side, we knew the Truth. We were completely vulnerable and dependent. We were open to receiving love and we freely gave love. We were not wrapped in fear or consumed by anxiety. We were completely in the present moment and didn't comprehend the concept of time. So what happened? Conditioning and domestication happened. We were unknowingly being taught by people that came before us to forget the Truths we knew and to embrace the false reality of how things are here.

Most of the planet is asleep, disconnected, and unconscious—it has been for thousands of years. This is why we live in a world with so many problems. To live in a world where we kill each other because we disagree is unconscionable. No one in their right mind would do that. To have fellow human beings starving amid abundant and available food and resources is unnecessary. To destroy the planet that hosts us and provides for us lacks logic. The process of thinking that runs rampant in this world is dysfunctional and could be diagnosed as sociopathic. I'm not saying this to be grandiose or to strike fear, it's simply the truth. The traits that society as a whole lives by and the processes in which determinations are made are profoundly flawed. Because of the unconscious, conditioned way of thinking that has been passed down from generation to generation, we are taught the same flawed ways that the previous generation was taught.

When we come into this world knowing we are safe, loved, and all is well, it's a huge adjustment to fit into a world that doesn't see things that way. It begins when we teach children to eat at dinner time, not when they're hungry. This is one small example of how we teach the next generation to ignore and deny messages their bodies are sending. We also teach that love is conditional. "When you do what I tell you, I'll give you positive feedback in the form of love. When you do things I don't want you to do, I'll give you negative feedback, so you don't feel love."

We're constantly pulling children out of moments of bliss and joy because of this concept called time, and we're making them do things that aren't joyful instead. For example, picture a child at play who is immersed in the present moment. We stop him, strap him into a car seat where he can't release his energy, and make him behave in a grocery store.

Have you ever noticed how long it takes children to understand the concept of time? Children can learn all types of ways to interact in the world at a very early age, but they are resistant to the concept of time. It takes years for them to learn, and yet it's taught multiple times every day. This is because living in the moment is a primal instinct with a profound sense of joy that's difficult to surrender.

By experiencing these constant "teachings", we begin to release what we know to be true and replace it with what society and our role models tell us. A foundational message is that we're not good enough. We can't trust our bodies or natural intuition; when we're in the moment and experiencing pure joy, it must end abruptly. We can't do what feels right; we must regularly do what feels wrong to us. As this is reinforced repeatedly, the only logical conclusion is that there's something wrong with us, the way we feel, our intuition, and what we want. Love is conditional on how much we change and do what others want us to do.

That's the bad news. Now, here's the good news.

These dysfunctional ways are merely belief systems, which are simply things that you agreed to believe in at some point in time. You can change them by deciding to believe something different.

Of course, it takes some focus to go into these belief systems, recognize which ones you formed and decide what you'd like to replace them with. It also takes reinforcement to create a new normal, building new neural pathways to the new way of thinking. But, here's more good news: It's not that difficult and it's completely worth it.

This is why awareness is so important, and is three quarters of the work. People stay stuck in old ways of Being because they're unaware. Once you're aware of a problem, there's a natural urge to want to fix it. We all want to be happy, but we don't always know what's blocking our path to experiencing it. Sometimes people can be aware of a problem but unwilling to change. That's their prerogative, but people usually *will* change once they've suffered enough, or perhaps they'll choose not to change in this life. We have free will and nothing can override it. Ultimately, it's our choice.

A large part of this book highlights our learned way of dysfunctional thinking; and how it doesn't work while directing us towards what does work. This book is not designed to teach you anything new, but to remind you of what you already know deep within. The words are pointing toward your innate way of Being. If something you read clicks with you, it means that you are remembering, not that you are learning. It took years to forget and be reprogrammed into a way of thinking that goes against your grain and doesn't make sense. It's much easier to remember a way of thinking that is natural to you and *does* make sense.

Chapter 5

Processing Information and Emotional Energy

It is important to understand the dynamics of thinking and feeling. From an energetic perspective, we can see how energy transmutes and gets trapped. In quantum physics, a thought can be measured as a unit of energy. So as a stimulus comes into our awareness, we instantly judge it as good or bad. This determines the vibration of energy that it transmutes into as an emotion. So if I watch my child score a goal, I judge it as good and it triggers a positive emotion. At the same time, the goalie's parent is judging this action as bad and it triggers a negative emotion. So we have a pattern: stimulus into thought into emotion. An emotion's job is to be felt. Once it's been felt, it can leave and transmute into a different form of energy. If it is stuffed down and not allowed to be felt, it's trapped and stays attached to us.

We generally don't stifle positive emotions because they're pleasurable, so we usually allow ourselves to feel them. The negative ones are the problem. We've been conditioned to not feel things that we consider uncomfortable. For years we have been unconsciously and consistently stuffing them, resulting in quite a buildup.

Now, what happens when energy is trapped? It begins to spin on itself within its container, gaining momentum and trying to escape. Energy doesn't sit still—it moves. This is why we lose our temper. This is why the amount of emotion that flies out when we open the hatch is usually disproportionate to the situation at hand. There's a large amount of stuffed emotion trying to get out, and it will take any exit route it can find.

Now that you understand the basics, we can focus on changing our process to have a more pleasurable experience here in this realm.

To have a more pleasurable experience, we must shift the way we're perceiving things. Our perception is our reality. When people perceive things as generally good, they don't generate as much negative energy as those who perceive things as generally bad. We can use our emotions as a red flag to let us know when we're judging something negatively. Once we're aware that we are doing this, we can choose to reframe the situation so that it doesn't trigger negative emotions. We don't have to lie to ourselves. We simply reframe the way we choose to look at a situation that doesn't leave us feeling like the victim, but in a way that either empowers us or allows us to accept the situation.

One example of this is driving. People who struggle with anger while driving have unconsciously developed a way of processing information negatively while on the road. They are the judge and jury for every situation that occurs, even though they don't have 90 percent of the information required to arrive at a fair conclusion. They take things personally when it has nothing to do with them. Let's say someone is driving too slowly and then speeds up when this person tries to pass them. The judge in their head determines they don't like this, which triggers a negative emotion. They might yell or honk the horn during the incident, but most of this anger is not only stuffed down, it's reinforced, and more is created around the incident. They either keep going over the story in their heads, or they tell others later and relive the incident. This creates more negative energy each time.

In situations like this, if we feel negativity, we need to slow ourselves down for a moment so we can deal with it differently. First, we can release the energy by allowing ourselves to feel the negative emotion. Don't think about what happened. Think about the physical sensations of what you're experiencing, such as tightness in the chest or pressure in the head and temples. Allow yourself to feel these sensations without judgment. A simple situation like traffic carries only 20 to 30 seconds worth of energy, so it shouldn't take too long. Once you've allowed the negative energy to be felt, it will transmute into something else and leave you. Now it's time to reframe the way you looked at the situation to begin reprogramming yourself to interact with life in a more enjoyable way.

Instead of believing the other driver intentionally singled you out to ruin your day for no apparent reason, look at the situation in another way. Perhaps the person was figuring out how to leave their spouse, or how they were going to handle a difficult situation with their child. Maybe a song on the radio evoked old memories and distracted them for a few moments. Have you ever done anything like that? Has your mind ever wandered while driving? Seriously, did you ever get into your car and say to yourself, "I'm going to find a random person on the road and begin to drive in a way that pisses them off as much as possible today"? Of course not. By reframing a situation to understand it wasn't about you, it removes the victim mentality and puts you in a better space. You're not the victim of someone on the road. You were near someone who was probably thinking of something else momentarily while driving. This is something we've all done and there's no reason to feel negative emotion.

You can invent an alternative possibility that is closer to the truth than how you originally perceived it. It must be something feasible that you can believe. Don't attempt to lie to yourself, your subconscious won't believe it and it won't shift anything. We are not lying to ourselves. We are reframing things hypothetically in a more realistic, positive way. Doing this helps prevent us from stuffing negative energy in the moment, as well as retraining our mind to view things in healthier ways down the road.

We can even reframe more extreme circumstances by consciously choosing to view them in healthier ways. You'll get better at it the more you practice. The main takeaway is that if you are feeling a negative emotion, there's usually another way to view it. Often, people defend their right to be upset with great intensity. But why defend the right to experience something you don't enjoy? Just because most people would be upset when someone hits their car and doesn't leave a note, doesn't mean that it's appropriate to get ticked off too. Getting upset isn't going to fix your car, and it's not going to prevent it from happening again. So how does the anger serve you? It doesn't.

Here are some ways to view the situation without a victim mentality. Perhaps it was a teenager who just got his license and was petrified over his parents' reaction, so he panicked. Or maybe it was an older person who didn't notice that her car made contact. It could have been someone in an abusive relationship who didn't want to take a beating over it. Who knows? You don't, and that's the point. It doesn't help matters to assume the worst. All it does is cause you to walk around with anger inside.

Let's get more specific about releasing negative emotion. The most common mistake people make when attempting to feel emotion is recreating the same emotion that you're attempting to release. It's important to understand your body doesn't know the difference between experiencing something and thinking about something. Your body generates the same toxins and energy either way. You can see this in the word *resentment*. It comes from the root word *sentir*, which means "to feel." So resentment literally means to feel again. When you walk around with resentment toward someone or something, you constantly feel the emotion surrounding it. And every time you feel it, you stuff more emotion around it. With this in mind, don't continue "telling the story" in your head as you're feeling emotion. You can use a story to conjure up a certain batch of stuffed emotion if you'd like, but as soon as you feel a physical sensation, you need to let go of the story.

Here's an example. I'm thinking about my childhood to release some trapped emotion and I remember a specific example of getting punished for something I didn't do. When I start feeling upset, this is the energy of emotion bubbling up. This is what I want to feel and release. I must immediately let go of the story I'm remembering and focus on the physical sensation, like feeling nauseous. My emotions can't hurt me, they just need to be felt. Now my heart is beating faster and I feel a pressure in my chest. It's okay. I'm all right. This energy is going up the back of my neck into my head now. It's very interesting because I never realized how much energy could travel throughout my body. Now, it's squeezing my temples, but I'm still okay.

It's nice to know that you can stop this process at your discretion. If it gets to be too much, or you simply have other things to do, you can stop the process of feeling whenever you want. You may have to respectfully demand that it stop by stating it with a firm intention, but you *can* stop it because you're in control. You've been stuffing emotions your whole life, so why would it be impossible to stop yourself from feeling it now?

In this last example, I'm discussing a trapped emotion around specific areas. While this could be extremely uncomfortable, it's usually manageable. There is another kind of trapped emotion that is more powerful and has more fear attached to it. This is the black abyss. There is no light because there is no love here. It is pure pain and lots of it! When you poke around deep inside, you come across a big batch of pain that seems overwhelming. It feels as if you allowed yourself to go into it, you'd never be able to make it out. You're not sure what would happen, but you wouldn't make it. Perhaps you think you'd go crazy or maybe implode. Who knows? It just feels like it's too much to handle and it's scary!

I stood at the edge of a cliff like this and decided that I wasn't willing to live the way I was living, so I didn't really care what happened. I would either come out the other side, or I'd spend the rest of my years in an institution, or I'd implode. It didn't really matter. What I *wasn't* going to do was continue living with it inside of me. So I went in, leaned forward, and fell off the cliff into a morass of pure pain. It hurt! I cried and it felt like my heart was being ripped from my chest. I stayed and felt it. I sobbed; I snot-bubbled; and I screamed into a pillow. Then I started hyperventilating. Twenty minutes later, as was lying on the floor going unconscious, I thought "I can't do this anymore." Suddenly, it stopped. I was both shocked and relieved. This is when I deeply understood that we are fully in charge of our own experiences. I had no idea that I could simply stop "feeling" whenever I wanted. I wish I had known that before I started, because I would have had more courage to make the initial leap.

Chapter 6

The Only Thing that Spiritual Law Cannot Override Is Free Will

This is an important spiritual truth: Free will is the only thing spiritual law cannot override. We have free will and our relationship with the Universe/God is based on this free will. The foundation for the relationship between Creator and Creation is Love, not control. The moment the Creator comes in and says you must do this or you must feel that because I know what's best for you, the relationship is shattered. The entire system falls apart, and the Universe would probably no longer exist because it breaks the fundamental principle on which everything is based: Love. We are the masters of our own fate. If we are to have a loving relationship with our Creator, it must be based in love which is a choice. We must be free to choose.

I came into spirituality through the door of recovery and I think addicts and alcoholics are good examples of this freedom of choice. To the outside world, it's obvious that stopping would be a good idea. Often, it's even obvious to the addict. So our all-powerful Creator could simply touch an addict's heart and remove the addiction. There...it's done. If the Creator could do this for all addicts, think of how much suffering would be minimized by this one act. So why doesn't a loving Creator simply do this? Because it would break the fundamental principle that everything is based on: Love. Controlling people is not love. You can't do something negative to achieve a positive outcome. If it's control, it's not unconditional love. If you love unconditionally, you can't control. Simple and true...it must be spiritual.

Chapter 7

Happiness

Let's look at the end goal. Happiness. You have to know where you're going in order to make the right turns to get there.

What's the point of self-development? Spirituality? They are ways to reconnect with the sense of safety that is deep inside us. From this sense of safety, we can begin to interact with life the way we should. Life is supposed to be an exciting adventure filled with all sorts of enjoyable growth experiences. We are here to expand into fuller and healthier versions of ourselves.

It is a fact that the Universe is constantly expanding. Like everything else, it is a sum of its parts. Therefore, if the Universe is expanding, it's a result of its parts expanding. Guess what you are? A part of the Universe. As you expand into a fuller version of yourself, the Universe expands. That is how important you are!

As we know, everything is energy. So, how do things expand? By putting more energy into them. Plants grow when they receive more energy in the forms of sunlight and water. People expand internally when they're exposed to and open up to more Love. We shine brighter and the reach of our warmth extends further. It's like a bonfire. The more fuel (Love), the larger the fire. We give fuel to what we want to expand and starve what we don't want.

If you would like to experience more happiness, focus your attention on it and it will expand. One of the best ways to do this is through gratitude. Gratitude is the action word of happiness, the verb. Focusing on what you're grateful for brings more attention (energy) to the happiness you already have within, thereby expanding it. As you are more aware of the happiness you have inside of you, it bubbles up closer to the surface which increases your experience of it. You notice it more, you enjoy the way it feels and continue to increase the attention on it, thereby bringing more and more to the surface.

Be conscious of the fact that happiness bubbles up from within. It isn't something outside of you. It's simply within you. One sure way to avoid happiness is to seek it. We tend to look for it externally. However, True happiness, which some people call joy, comes from within. It can be as simple as deciding that happiness is your state of Being regardless of what's happening externally. People have found peace and happiness within themselves on death row, in a hospital bed, or living on the streets.

Happiness is not contingent on your circumstances. If it were, no one would ever have it in this ever-changing reality. This is a great way to gain perspective on things, including happiness. Let's play God for a moment, hypothetically of course. So, imagine you were God and you created an entire world with all your creations on it. One species was very special because you gave them free will and they could make their own choices. Of course, you love your creations because they are a part of you; just like you love your children, the business you built, the art you expressed, or anything else you created. There's an innate love for these things simply because they are your creations. Would you create a world where your creations were required to attain certain status, wealth, and possessions? External things which are often unnecessary to live a happy life? Also, would you have this be required of them within an ever-changing reality? Of course not. If they were lucky enough to acquire it all and get everything in place, things would soon change and obstruct the very things that they worked so hard to establish for their happiness. That would be cruel; and it makes no sense to set up a cruel system for creations that you love.

While you're still in the "God seat," would it make more sense to design a system where happiness comes from within? Then, your very special creations only need to open to the love and joy inside of them and interact with the ever-changing reality in a fun, exciting way. They could use all the possibilities of experiences, goals, and acquisitions as a means of finding and expressing the happiness inside of them in their own way. That sounds like a reality I would create for something I love. Of course, you have given them free will, so they have the right to *not* do that if they so choose. You had to give them free will; otherwise, your relationship with them would have been based on control, not love, and everything must be based in love because you love your creations.

Do you notice when you take a giant step backwards and gain perspective, suddenly things begin to get clearer? The way we were conditioned to find happiness externally doesn't work. It simply doesn't make sense. It doesn't hold water. The old idea of going to school, getting good grades, landing a job, having a family, buying a house, and *then* you'll be happy, simply doesn't work. Of course, if you open up to your own happiness and *then* do those things, they can be an expression of your happiness. There is no happy destination at the end of an unhappy road. You must walk the happy road to arrive at the happy destination.

What is happiness compared to momentary pleasure? As I explained, happiness is derived internally. However, we can experience moments of pleasure through external things such as eating something tasty, taking part in activities we enjoy, and purchasing something we want. Momentary pleasure exists and there's a place for it, but we shouldn't confuse it with True happiness because it's fleeting and dependent on external circumstances. It's merely an attempt to fill a hole in ourselves; it's like trying to fill a hole in the earth with the thought of dirt, it simply has no substance.

Chapter 8

Filling the Hole

Let's examine the idea of filling the hole in more detail. There is a theory that all of humankind's problems derive from its separation from Source. It's also been famously said by French mathematician Blaise Pascal, "All of humanity's problems stem from man's inability to sit quietly in a room alone." If we are disconnected from who and what we are, our reason for being here, and our Source of Love, peace, fulfillment, and joy...well, no wonder we can't sit quietly in a room alone. Stillness is where we can connect to our Source, but when we're disconnected it's also where the pain of that disconnection bubbles up and is felt.

I remember my first solo plane flight as a passenger after I woke up spiritually. I brought many things with me to distract myself and pass the time, but I didn't use any of them. I was content sitting still, looking out the window, or simply sitting there quietly. I didn't understand why until I spoke with a friend. After relating my experience, he said, "Yes, it's the first time you flew with someone you liked." The light bulb went off and I realized it was true. I liked myself. I had peace inside instead of anguish. I didn't have to distract myself from the pain I used to feel inside anymore. It was peaceful to be still!

If we take a close look at society, we see many unhealthy ways people try to fill the hole they instinctively feel within themselves. Addictions such as alcohol, legal and illegal drugs, cigarettes, and overeating are addictions that attempt to fill the hole. Many people use relationships, sex, shopping, working out, television, and social media to distract themselves from the hole they feel when they are still. By numbing themselves with drugs, alcohol, unhealthy behaviors, and using fast-paced living and distraction techniques, most people can avoid dealing with the fact that they are unhappy and unfulfilled in life.

The world is experiencing a spiritual shift. The way we've done things up till now doesn't work anymore. Change is necessary for the evolution of our species and this spiritual shift is trying to be birthed into the world. We must find another way of Being if we are going to survive—one based on Love for one another. This is why feeling uncomfortable about our separation from Source is becoming more prevalent. More and more people are unable to shove it back down, and pretend they don't feel it anymore. It's becoming too powerful, and the need to evolve and change is pushing its way to the surface.

There are two choices: You can close yourself and stuff it down as much as possible through numbing and distraction methods; or you can open and connect to our Source.

These are the same two choices that are the foundation of how we live. In all experiences and situations, we can choose to either open or close. If we open, we expand and grow: becoming more of ourselves, aligning with our natural way of Being, and resulting in more happiness. If we close, we build walls: tightening, constricting, becoming a lesser version of ourselves, and resulting in more suffering.

Opening isn't always easy. In fact, many times it's downright hard, but it is always simple and effective. Joy, peace, and happiness are on the other side waiting for you to open up to them. Do your best to open, even when it's hard, because the alternative is continued suffering. The payoff is lasting peace wrapped in a blanket of love you've never felt before!

Chapter 9

Fulfillment

Fulfillment deserves a moment of clarification under the microscope. Fulfillment is when you are connected to your inner happiness, following your personal path in the energies of love and joy, and feel the fullness of that hole being no longer empty. Fulfillment is the inner sensation you feel as your "cup runneth over," as you give from the overflow. It is the sheer bliss of Love enveloping you while the breath of God flows through you like a flute making beautiful music. It is what you feel when you are doing what you love simply for the joy of it and completely unattached to a specific outcome. Doing what you love has its own reward. It's called fulfillment.

You see, fulfillment isn't externally based either. It's not what you feel when you attain something. It's what you feel while you're doing what you're supposed to be doing, simply because that's who you are. Of course you receive accolades, material things, and achievements, but that's not why we do it. We do it for the joy and fulfillment of the process and who we become along the way. The external things are simply expressions of the fulfillment inside and represent the joy we experienced in the process of our achievements. They are merely external symbols of the internal reality.

Chapter 10

Spiderweb with Goodness

I must touch on my spiderwebbing with goodness mentality. I've noticed during my spiritual walk that I'll never fully comprehend all the good that happens when I'm in alignment with spirituality. Things tend to connect to other things and enhance more aspects of my life than I ever could have imagined. It's like a ripple on the water that is continually expanding.

There have been times in my life and my client's lives when wonderful things happen while working on something else. One example is working on boundaries with a difficult person. The process starts with learning how to set boundaries with a person because the relationship is not healthy. The obvious positive result is that the situation gets resolved in one way or another and it's no longer an issue. However, when I'm doing the work on myself, it spiderwebs outward with goodness. I'm healthier in all my relationships: with my friends, family, co-workers, children, etc. Because my relationships are better, I'm experiencing a happier life and spreading love to more and more people, including strangers. When I set boundaries and ask for what I need, my self-esteem rises along with my self-love. Then I'm more capable of being in a healthy romantic relationship and handling my business dealings in a more effective, meaningful way. Because of these changes, I'm more motivated and I start believing that I can achieve anything I want to achieve. I also feel closer to my Higher Power which gives me the courage to work on my faith and put more trust into something I don't fully understand. I'm in the flow and others feel this flow. When they see the changes in my life, it inspires them to begin their journey. If Glenn can do it, they can too!

You get the point. One positive action links into another area that I didn't even know was going to be affected. Sometimes I'll handle a situation so well that I'll wonder how I did it. That was awesome! I'll look back and see a spiderweb of goodness that started 15 years ago attaching to one thing, then another, then another, and ends up helping with the situation I was just in. At these times, I'm humbled and honored to be part of whatever is happening. It's bountiful, joyful, and wonderful beyond my comprehension. I simply love it!

PART 2

SPIRITUAL TOOLS

Chapter 11

Starving What We Don't Want

Just as we feed what we *do* want, we must starve what we *don't* want. For example, if you don't want to be in a relationship, you could simply starve it and eventually it will end. Of course, that's not a very healthy or respectful way to end a relationship, but it would work in most situations.

If you want a fire to die out, simply deny its source of energy by not adding fuel. If you've determined that someone is not a healthy choice for you, simply stop putting energy into keeping them in your life. One day, you will wake up and realize that you haven't spoken with this person in months. How did that happen? When did that happen? It doesn't matter, it simply did. These methods require some responsibility and consciousness. It's rude to ignore people in many situations. Give some people the courtesy and respect of having a conversation, while others will simply fall away. Many of my past surface relationships fell away with no hard feelings and no abrupt ending. It was just organic when I allowed it to happen.

To regain control over your thought processes, you don't have to fight your ego. That's like saying, "Don't think of the color red." Of course the first thing you'll think of is the color red. What you need to do is feed the new way of thinking and starve the old by not putting any energy into it.

This is a matter of creating new neural pathways in the brain. If a neural pathway is not used, it will begin to disintegrate. As you reinforce a new one, it gains momentum and strength, eventually becoming the new way of thinking. Reinforce the one you want by choosing to think, behave, and act consciously in a positive way, and then starve the old way of thinking without a fight.

Chapter 12

The Replacement Technique

It's difficult to stop thinking of something once it's a conditioned thought, so replacing the thought is a more effective way of dealing with it. I call it the replacement technique.

First, identify the thought that needs to change. Perhaps you're constantly thinking of a break-up with an ex-boyfriend or ex-girlfriend. Or you get angry whenever you have to deal with a specific person like your ex-spouse, or an institution like your cell phone company. Or you get stressed whenever you have to go somewhere, like the grocery store to shop or return an item.

Next, figure out a healthy way to view the situation that doesn't trigger a negative emotion and propel you into the victim mentality. With a relationship ending, you could determine that you keep thinking of your ex-lover because you miss the intimacy in the relationship. Often, losing your best friend, your confidant, the person you shared your life with is the loss of an intimate connection. The only thing that we can depend upon all the time, for anything we need, is our Source. It is our Source of everything, including abundance, intimacy, unconditional love, peace, and joy. So every time you think of that person, take a moment to connect with your Source. Feel the love and the contentment in the stillness of the moment. Take a breath, center yourself, and feel the calmness and intimacy of Love from your Source. You can do this 300 times a day! When you learn to derive your sense of unconditional love from your Source, rather than another person, you will stop feeling lonely. You will stop longing for intimacy because you will get used to having it at your fingertips whenever you want. This also greatly increases your own self-love and reduces the neediness that often comes with romantic relationships. You don't need someone else to fulfill you. You are already fulfilled. Now you can open up and share your fullness with someone without trying to get something in return to complete you.

Even grocery shopping can be a very stressful situation. If your brain is telling you that you hate shopping because there are always so many people who get in your way and behave rudely, it's time to stop, center yourself, and reframe your thinking. Choose a healthier perspective. For example, you can tell yourself that it only takes 90 minutes out of your life to perform this necessary task for your family to eat for the entire week. That's 9,990 minutes your family get to enjoy and live off of what took you only 90 minutes to acquire. That's not a bad trade! By staying focused on your breathing and using this as a learning opportunity on how to stay in the moment and not allow your circumstances to determine your happiness, you could look back on this as one of the most profound spiritual practices of your life.

Of course, these are just a couple of examples. You may have to seek the help of a professional or simply another positive person to develop a way of looking at a situation that feeds you instead of drains you. Once you have this new thought form, it's time to implement it. The largest piece of this process is learning not to discuss or argue the points of this change inside your head. Don't argue with your ego about it. Your ego is used to the old way of thinking and wants to go back to it, so don't get into a debate about it. To help with this, make a plan.

The ego doesn't understand long-term thinking, so when you're not in a situation, it's the best time to design a course of action for when you are in the situation. Your ego won't argue when it's not happening now, it's only good at controlling you in the moment. Take time to think things through ahead of time, and then stick to it at the time of implementation, consciously bypassing the arguing ego.

This is a wonderful process for creating new habits like beginning an exercise regimen. Determine what you're going to do ahead of time while the ego isn't sticking its nose into things. I'm not exercising this weekend; I'm just planning my routine for next week. This way your ego is at rest and not looking for danger because nothing is "happening" when you're in your planning mode. Then put your plan on the schedule and make a personal commitment to adhere to it—no matter what your ego says when the time comes.

Don't allow yourself to discuss your plan, revamp your plan, or skip your plan for a certain amount of time—let's say two weeks, depending on what works for you. Repeat after me: "For two weeks, I will follow through with my plan, even if it's the biggest mistake of my life. If that's the case, I'll be a complete fool for two weeks, then I'll make the necessary adjustments at the end of the two weeks. However, I'm not going to discuss it now. I'm not changing it for any reason. I thought it out when I was making my plan, and that's good enough. If I made a mistake, I'll live with it until I fix it on my reassessment date. I made a commitment to myself and, out of self-respect, I will keep this commitment." Making this personal commitment will increase your self-esteem and success while you develop a new habit.

The main point here is to create a new way of thinking ahead of time and commit to doing it. Don't get into a chess match with your ego when the time comes to implement it. Simply trust the reasoning you used when you were still and thinking clearly to determine how you'd handle a situation when it arises.

Chapter 13

Three Steps to Solving Any Problem

You can solve any problem by using a three-step process. When you simplify, you get closer to the Truth. Here is the overview:

1. **Identify the problem.** Get clear on the real underlying problem. It may be different than how it appears on the surface. Go inside and ask the question over and over, going deeper each time. Listen to your heart, not your head.

2. **Find the solution.** Look into how others have solved similar problems, gather information if necessary, and look at it from a place of Love not frustration.

3. **Implement the solution.** You need to follow through with action, which is usually the most difficult step. Following through with the solution is paramount!

If hunger is your problem, you can drive to the store, select your food, pay for it, load it in your car, drive home, cook it, plate the food, and eat it. If you miss just one step in this process, the whole plan will fall apart. You need clear steps and the ability to accomplish each one.

Job issues are a common concern so we'll use the process in that example. Let's go through step by step:

1. **Identify the problem** — If your job is a problem, break it down to exactly what is bothering you about it. Is it the relationship with your boss? Getting along with co-workers? The commute? The daily activities of your job? Be specific and identify the parts you like and the parts you don't like about your job situation.

2. **Find the solution** — Do you need to set boundaries with your boss or co-workers? Be more loving to co-workers? Find a job closer to home doing the same thing? Find a job doing something different? Again, be specific in your solution as it addresses the one or multiple issues.

3. **Implement the solution** — Set time on your schedule to have a talk with the boss about your relationship stating that you'd like it to be better. Reach out to co-workers in whatever way is necessary. Begin job searching for something closer or performing different tasks. Or perhaps start your own business doing something you love on the side. Whatever the solution is—implement it!

Often, people waste time by saying they should be able to handle things on their own, but they never get anywhere. You don't have to do it alone. You weren't meant to do it alone. That's why we have an innate inner desire for community and acceptance. We need each other. Talk things out and ask for help—it helps!

This simple process works because it slows down the mind and allows you to use your thinking capabilities in a logical, problem-solving way without all the emotion that clouds your vision. Get clear on the problem, identify the solution, and then implement it. The process is so simple and effective, it must be spiritual!

Chapter 14

Simplify

If you want to get closer to the Truth—simplify. If you want to get farther from the Truth—complicate. In this book, we will step out of complexity and step into the simplicity of Truth.

The more complicated things are, the more places false information can hide. Think about two of the most complicated systems that are in place: government and health insurance. Now look at how many problems are caused by their complexity.

The same applies to our own lives. When we complicate things, we get further from the Truth. We need to simplify them. When you're feeling overwhelmed, it's often because there are several issues all tied into one making it seem complicated. We're incapable of handling four different things at once. However, we can handle one thing at a time. The first thing to do is to simplify by separating the issues into several smaller issues, and then deal with one at a time. Feeling overwhelmed often leads to shutting down. Then things usually get worse because more things hop onto the pile and the four-issue pile becomes a six-issue pile. It's important to simplify and take one step at a time.

Often people feel like they hate their job and therefore the solution is to quit. Sometimes this is the best move but oftentimes it's not. If you slow down and ask yourself exactly what you hate about your job, you may find out that you actually like your job activities and almost all the people you work with; but the fact that your boss has been talking to you with complete disrespect is bothering you tremendously. Perhaps the solution is to set a healthy boundary around the way you are spoken to. If you attempt to set a boundary and find that your boss is incapable of respecting it, you may decide to look for another job. Or you may find your boss actually accepts the boundary. Believe it or not, this happens more often than not. Most people don't enjoy treating other people poorly. It's often an unconscious pattern that gets better when pointed out.

Another trick here is to not come to conclusions without trying things first. When this type of issue comes up, people love believing they know what the boss will do, or that they've tried setting boundaries and it didn't work, when in fact, they either haven't set a "real boundary" or they didn't enforce it correctly. Setting a boundary needs to be done properly and consciously to work. More to come in further chapters on healthy boundaries.

Simplifying is the same mentality that's used in recovery and other places with the slogan "One day at a time." We can always handle one thing at a time, one moment at a time, and even one day at a time. However, we can't handle everything all at once. As absurd as that sounds out loud, we often attempt to do it without even realizing it. Separate things, simplify them; and as you get closer to the Truth, the easier things will become. Divide and conquer!

Chapter 15

Guidance System

Everyone Is born with their own personal guidance system to use while we're here on earth. I call it God's Positioning System (GPS). It tells us when we're heading in the right direction and when we're not. I also call it a Joy-O-Meter (JOM), but that acronym isn't as clever as GPS.

When you are heading in the right direction, you experience joy, happiness, excitement, enthusiasm, and other positive emotions. When you are heading in the wrong direction, you experience frustration, unhappiness, anger, sadness, and other bad feelings. If you were meant to do accounting, you would enjoy doing accounting. So why would you be "meant" to do something that didn't bring you joy?

When you enjoy something, you're much better at it than people who don't enjoy it—simply because you enjoy applying yourself to it. Tom Brady is a great example of this. He *loves* football. He's not the most talented or physically gifted quarterback who ever played the game, but he is arguably one of the best players who has ever played the position. This is because he loves it. He loves learning, practicing, becoming better, watching game film, and everything else related to football. His commitment level is so high because he genuinely enjoys football; it doesn't feel like work to him. You could never become as good as he is at something if you don't enjoy it. You simply wouldn't do the extra work because it's not fun.

When I work with anyone in my personal or business life, I always look for a passion for their craft. A person who is passionate about their profession or craft, whether a chiropractor, acupuncturist, plumber, golf instructor, life coach, marketing guru, or ditch digger, is going to be 10 times better than someone who is just doing a job to earn a paycheck. The passionate person will take the time to find out what that asterisk means at the bottom of the page of one of their textbooks or develop more streamlined and effective ways of doing things related to their job.

When you're in alignment with your passion, you experience joy and feel like you are positioned correctly in life. When you're feeling frustrated and unhappy, it's a sign that you aren't positioned correctly and need to make adjustments.

I use a bowling alley to give a visual for this lesson. In bowling alleys, they often have rubber bumpers that you can put down in the gutters for children learning to bowl. It's impossible to get a "gutterball" because the bumpers keep the ball from dropping In. Life is like this—you can't get a gutterball! All is well; you are loved and it will all work out in the end.

Visualize for a moment: the ball is rolling down the alley, getting too far to the right and then to the left, gently bouncing off the bumpers when an adjustment is necessary. This is how life is supposed to work. We're supposed to get a little nudge when we're veering off our path to help keep us in the center. If we make these slight adjustments when we experience uncomfortability, life goes pretty smoothly. However, instead of making the adjustments, people often stay in the same conditions, heading in the same wrong direction for extended periods of time. Now visualize the bowling ball rubbing up against that bumper, grinding all the way down the alley. You can almost feel the rubber bumper up against your skin with more and more pressure causing an immense amount of pain. This is what happens when we don't make the adjustments necessary towards our own joy. Life becomes more and more uncomfortable. Not as a punishment but as a guidance system attempting to tell us: Happiness is not in this direction. I love you. I want what's best for you. Please make an adjustment so that you can be happy.

The Universe can't reward behavior that veers away from happiness. Otherwise, how would we know where our happiness lies? The system is designed for us to feel discomfort when we're heading in the wrong direction and joy when we're heading in the right direction—it's that simple.

PART 3

LIVING WITH THE EGO

Chapter 16

Ego Explained

This brings us to understanding the Truth behind the "two of us." There are two voices inside your head: one is constantly chatting it up, and then there is the *awareness* that there's a voice inside your head constantly chatting it up. You're made up of two aspects from two different realms, each with different characteristics; so it only makes sense that, to some degree, there are two of you. However, one is "real," and one is not. It's important to identify with the "real" one while being aware of the other one.

The voice chatting it up is often referred to as the ego. This is the mind-made self, who you think you are in this Temporal Realm. The *awareness* is the True self, the eternal self.

The mind-made ego is a useful aspect of yourself because It has a purpose. Why would everyone on the planet have an ego and identify with it if it weren't useful in some way? What's its original purpose? To warn you of possible danger.

The ego's job is to protect you. So if something were set up to protect you, would it be looking for happy, joyful things? Of course, not. It would be looking for dangerous things, so that it could warn you and you could protect yourself.

The problem is that we've become so overly identified with that voice in our head warning us of things, that we think it's us. We think that is our voice, that if a thought passes through, we must be thinking it and there must be truth to it. The fact is, we're not supposed to believe everything it says.

If you set up a motion-activated light in your front yard, it can help warn you of an approaching intruder. If the light goes on, you can peer outside to see what set off the motion detector. If you see a bunny hopping around, then you can relax, fully assured there is no impending danger and let go of the fact that the light came on. However, if you see strangers with guns slung over their shoulders, then you have good reason to become concerned for your physical safety and react appropriately.

The problem is that the ego doesn't have the ability to distinguish what is real danger and what is possible danger. That's not its job. Its job is to continually keep an eye open and transmit a thought. The ego has no decision-making capabilities; it's just a warning system. It is your job to take and interpret the information coming in, and then arrive at a conclusion. Is this something that demands attention or something you can dismiss as inconsequential? Then you can act in alignment with that decision.

If you over-identify with your ego, you will always believe the warnings of danger. You will never feel safe. You will be fearful about what could happen next and how it will affect you and your loved ones. This is unconscious living.

What if I lose my job? What if my partner falls in love with someone else? What if my child gets hurt? What if I get in an accident? What if I don't have time to pick up the groceries? What if I don't finish the laundry today? All these thoughts run incessantly through your head causing anxiety and fear over things that most likely won't happen. And if they did, most of them are inconsequential. However, you don't know that because you're so identified with thoughts that are constantly triggering anxiety and defensive actions within your body.

Living in constant stress puts enormous strain on our bodies, especially our immune system. Your body doesn't know whether you're actually in physical danger or not. It simply feels fear in the form of anxiety and begins to react accordingly.

When fear is triggered, the body begins to send blood and energy to the major muscle groups to induce the fight-or-flight response, thereby robbing other areas of the body from much needed nutrients. There is much data to back up the fact that living under regular stress affects the body negatively in many ways. Listed here are the different systems that are said to be affected by living in elevated stress levels:

- **Immune system**
- **Sexuality and reproductive system**
- **Muscular system**
- **Digestive system**
- **Respiratory and cardiovascular systems**
- **Central nervous and endocrine systems**

Other than these systems being affected, you're fine! As you can see, living under constant stress affects major aspects of your health.

This is one of the reasons why that egoic voice is so detrimental when it is completely identified with. The other is what it does to us mentally. If we are constantly experiencing fear-based thoughts, our mental outlook is fearful and defensive. We are walking through life in constant fear.

Most conversations in everyday life reflect this. If you look closely, most conversations are to prove the way we're looking at things is the right way, thereby giving ourselves a sense of security and safety in being right. This is a form of attack and defend. Many conversations aren't about listening and exchanging ideas, they are about defending why your idea is correct.

Of course you see this play out in politics a lot. Neither side is concerned about focusing on the solution and working together, they are focused on proving the other side wrong and/or their side right. There is no focus on discussing a real solution because that's not the goal. The goal is to be right and therefore acquire more power to do things that they think will bring them even more power.

We tend to point the finger at politics and say that's the problem with the world, when the politics of our society are simply a reflection of us as a whole. If we weren't doing it ourselves in our own lives, on a smaller scale, it would be intolerable at the political level. If people went on television and argued instead of working towards a solution, we would turn the channel and not even contemplate voting for anyone involved in such an exchange.

However, it's become so commonplace and accepted in our culture that we lean into it.

Not only do we watch them, but most of society picks sides and takes part on a smaller scale in their own lives. Never noticing that there is no attempt at working together towards a solution. Instead everyone is arguing about who's right and who's wrong in an attempt to be right and acquire more power.

If we stop acting like this in our own lives on smaller scales, it'll be reflected back to us less on a larger scale. We must BE the change we wish to see. It starts with us.

We need to look closely into the dynamics of our conversations and behaviors to see things like this playing out. We are so conditioned to dysfunctional ways, we don't pick up on them at first glance. Slowing down and dissecting *what* you do and *why* you do it will give you the clarity you desire.

If you notice that you're late for an appointment, there are two ways to act. One is unconsciously and stressful while the other is productive and peaceful. Here are the two ways:

1. You can panic, run, grab your keys, shooting out the door to get into the car, then remembering that you forgot your phone or wallet, then running back in the house to get them, tripping along the way and almost falling, only to become more stressed because now you're even more late.

2. You can take a moment to breathe and center yourself, literally taking in one calming breath and letting it out, reminding yourself that all is well. Then you can consciously think: what do I need to grab before I go? Wallet, phone, keys. You get them calmly. You walk briskly, but centered, to the car and go.

One way, you tend to create more problems and experience the situation under stress and the other way you stay calm and peaceful which allows you to be more conscious and effective in the situation.

We must begin to understand we have a choice in how to act and what we feel. If something goes in a way that we don't like, it's not mandatory to feel stress and anxiety over it. We have a tendency to do that because we believe our ego's thoughts when it says something's wrong. As we become more conscious, we can pause, and then decide how to act in a situation instead of reacting unconsciously.

Our ego is fine, it has a job to do. If we let it do that job without allowing it to run us and push us into stress responses on a regular basis, everything is okay.

There is a tendency to deny or fight against things that we deem as "bad" in the world. This is true in the unconscious world and can also be true in what we consider the conscious or spiritual world. In the past there have been attempts to deny the body, the mind, and natural desires, blaming each of them for our disconnect with the spiritual realm.

However, we are spiritual Beings having a human experience. To deny the Truth of either aspect of ourselves causes problems. If you deny you're spiritual at the core, then you'll be lacking the peace, serenity, joy and fulfillment that being connected to Source provides. If you deny your humanity, or parts of it, suffering such as pain, anger, constant stress, and loneliness will enter your experience.

Understand yourself, make conscious choices instead of allowing the unconscious patterns to run your life and you'll realize you have much more power over your own happiness than you ever thought possible.

Chapter 17

The Trick of the Ego

In many parts of the world, we are fortunate there isn't much physical danger in everyday life. But the ego still wants to do its job and warn us of possible danger. When the ego is in control, it constantly warns us and often triggers unrealistic fears.

Case in point: Often, people are stuck in unhealthy relationships because the ego triggers fear and says, "You can't leave this relationship. What if you can't find someone else? Then you'll be alone. What if the next person is worse?" If you listen closer, the ego is really saying, "Don't leave this relationship because you might end up unhappy." But you're already unhappy because you're in an unhealthy relationship!

The ego is warning you to not do something because you might experience something you're already experiencing! How insane is that? Many people will listen to the ego and stay in a miserable relationship.

If you decide to leave, worst case scenario, you have a 50/50 shot at finding a healthy relationship. On the spiritual path, it's a lot higher than that. However, we'll use this example to keep things realistic for the thinking mind. So if you left, you might find a healthy relationship. But if you stay, your odds are 99 percent that it's not going to get better. I'd rather take the 50/50 odds that things could get better than settle for the 1 percent chance—thank you very much!

Do you see how the ego tries to protect you from experiencing suffering in the future, but it doesn't pay attention to the suffering you're experiencing right now? It says: "Don't do this because you might end up experiencing exactly what you're experiencing now." This is how we know the ego is a warning device that *we* should be in control of. It is not capable of reasoning and decision making. That is not its job, it's ours. We need to make conscious decisions and not allow a warning device to determine our actions based in fear.

There is nothing "wrong" with our bodies, our minds, our egos, our innate desires, or anything else that we've been blessed with by a Source far more intelligent than us. Sometimes we can be controlled by things we're supposed to control, and that's a problem. All you parents out there can try a little experiment: Allow your kids to do whatever they want, whenever they want, for an entire day or even a week. Allow them to determine how things should happen in their lives and your life as well. They don't have the same decision-making capabilities that you do. They haven't lived and experienced consequences like you have. There will be issues. This is why parents run the household. You've lived, learned, and developed decision-making capabilities that your kids and your ego don't have. So don't give the decision-making capabilities to someone or something incapable of making decisions.

It's fine for your ego to warn you of danger, but it's not okay to let it control you and push you into a life of stress and suffering.

Chapter 18

Complaining

The ego has been controlling how we think and what we do for the last 5,000 years. There have also been a lot of problems during this time. It's time we began to understand the ego, the way it works, and how to regain control over our lives. We don't have to spend a lot of time trying to beat down our ego. All we need to do is to connect and identify with the Truth of who we are and understand that our mind-made self is just a collection of identities that we slip into to play different roles in our lives.

Many people do habitual things that feed the ego in a way that they don't fully understand. This is why people tend to keep doing them, even when they're not healthy behaviors. For example, when people complain, they are subconsciously inferring that they wouldn't do it that way if it were up to them. They are also subconsciously inferring that they are better than the person or situation they are complaining about. This causes a sense of separation between them and what they're complaining about, putting them above the other person or situation in a "better than" position. In this way, complaining is simply stroking the ego to feel better.

Eckhart Tolle uses the example of ordering soup that is served to you cold, not hot.

> **Complaint**: This soup is cold, but it's supposed to be hot. Who is cooking back there? Don't they know how to serve soup?

Non-complaint: Excuse me, could I get the soup heated, please?

The complaint is searching for the "better than" position. The non-complaint simply addresses the problem without blame or ego-stroking.

We do this habitual ego stroking to feel just a little better. It works on a surface level that is never satisfied because we must constantly feed it. Complaining actually takes on an addictive energy because of its constant need for "a fix." If complaining is the lone way someone feels good about themselves, there's only so long they can go without falling into a deep depression or feeding their ego by complaining.

Now I'll give you an example of how tricky your ego can be. Next time you notice someone complaining, is your first instinct to judge or criticize them for complaining? That's complaining too. Catch it and choose something different!

In contrast, if we connect to who we truly are (not our ego) and function from there, we always know we're good enough. We're filled with love, peace, and the knowingness that all is well and that we are loved beyond measure. Living from this place is existing in a constant state of contentment and safety all the time. Even if we experience some things we don't enjoy in this life, we can simply take appropriate action to correct the situation while connected to an underlying current of peace that is always there.

Chapter 19

The Sacred Pause

Most of the time, we are living from a reactionary state instead of a conscious state. When someone asks a question, we unconsciously feel we must answer them immediately. When something happens, we react immediately. Often this is unnecessary and leads to many mistakes, mishandled situations, and rushed answers.

There is a very useful tool to help deal with this. It's called the sacred pause. In a conversation, it can be as short as a second or two, just enough to stop the brain from spitting out an unconscious response to whatever stimuli has been presented. If you give the brain just a moment, it can formulate an actual thought based on the information provided instead of a preconceived response to the general type of question asked.

In the beginning it will feel awkward to us, like people are waiting and wondering why we're not answering them. A split second in real time goes by slowly in our minds because we're used to reacting so quickly. Generally, people won't even notice it in most situations. Let's also examine what it looks like if someone notices that you're pausing and thinking before answering. It looks like you're putting thought into what they said before you respond. If someone gives you a hard time, you can simply tell them you wanted to think about their question and give them an honest, thought-out answer. Who can argue with that? Most people are impressed and grateful for this type of response since it's so rare.

There are numerous situations where people simply don't need to know your answer instantly, and would even prefer a thoughtful response. Begin to introduce new phrases in your life to help implement your pause such as:

- When do you need to know?
- Can I get back to you?
- Do you need an answer now?
- Can I look into it and let you know tomorrow?

These are helpful questions that can give you the space to answer people in an appropriate way. This will prevent many difficulties such as double bookings, and "yes" answers to things that you simply don't want to do once you have assessed them.

This is why there's so much being taught about mindfulness, being in the present moment, living in the Now, etc. Everyone is teaching it because it's necessary. Society is moving so quickly and unconsciously that we're not in control of the answers that are coming out of our mouths in everyday situations. We must slow down, become more conscious in our lives, and live with purpose and intention.

So, pause first and answer second. It's a simple tool that can make a huge impact on your life!

Chapter 20

Pain Pushes Until Pleasure Pulls

I'm sure it comes as no surprise when I say there's a lot of pain in this world. The reason there's a lot of pain is because there's a lot of change that's necessary for our own well-being and happiness. The Universe doesn't need us to learn through pain. However, it's usually the only thing that captures our attention enough to induce the type of self-reflection and surrender necessary to break out of the unconscious belief patterns that have been running the world for so long. Unfortunately, it's considered "normal" for people to experience pain, unhappiness, and live unfulfilling lives. Mood-enhancing drugs (legal and illegal) and a variety of addictive behaviors have become accepted ways to mask the constant levels of discomfort that people experience daily.

This is why such extreme pain is necessary to induce large change. Alcoholics and drug addicts are the most obvious examples of this. They "hit bottom" by experiencing a tremendous amount of pain through the breakdown of foundational parts of their lives, losing family, friends, career, etc. Through this suffering, they are pushed in the direction of surrender and change. Some surrender and open to change and some, unfortunately, attempt to self-medicate more and more to excess, culminating in an earlier transition.

At the end of the day, our path is to grow and become better, happier versions of ourselves. The entire Universe is expanding and growing. It's against our nature to stay stuck, unhappy, and unfulfilled. We experience pain to push us toward our destiny of happiness.

The next time you're feeling a painful situation, don't ask why it's happening to you. Ask yourself what the situation is trying to teach you. How can you grow from this? Assume you are loved and that the entire Universe in conspiring for your benefit and happiness. Look at painful situations through those eyes. It may take some practice, but eventually you'll cease being a victim and become the victor of your own life.

After breaking out of the pain pattern, you can learn in a different way, one without the extreme suffering. By reflecting on yourself and making the necessary adjustments when you feel uncomfortable, there will be less pain and more pleasure. Put more consciousness into what feels good and why it feels good, and you will learn from your successes.

It's exciting and fun to learn and grow! When we get in the flow of what brings us joy, we can learn through pleasure instead of pain. I often pray: "Teach me my lessons easy." I try to keep my head on a swivel, constantly making slight adjustments while living healthy and making expansive, conscious choices in my life. This way the pain is minimized, the joy is maximized, and life is the happy, fulfilling experience it should be!

Chapter 21

Fear of the Future

Living in anxiety for the future or regret about the past are conditioned behaviors. They aren't natural; they're not our "Truth." They don't make sense, and yet almost everyone experiences them regularly and considers it normal. This is why I don't aspire to be "normal." I don't feel what society considers normal to be anything I'd like to experience—it's actually what I'm trying to avoid.

Let's look at anxiety first for a moment. How does fear about what may hypothetically happen in the future benefit us? It simply doesn't. It has no benefits at all. We can plan things and attempt to make the best decisions based on the information we have at the moment; however, attaching fear to it only hurts us.

When we allow fear to live within us it expands, taking over our thought processes and controlling our lives. Start with something small and you'll realize how useless anxiety is. When you worry about the future, you're bringing more negative energy into the situation and making it even more likely to go in the direction you don't want. You're literally putting energy toward what you don't want to happen. Universal law doesn't understand "for" or "against," it simply understands the subject. When Mother Teresa was asked to go to an anti-war rally, she said, "No, but if you have a pro-peace rally, I'll be the first one there." She wasn't considered "New Age" but she understood the spiritual law that surpasses labels. She understood that if you put energy toward war, it doesn't matter if it is anti or pro…it is still energy toward war. In this way, stop putting energy toward what you don't want to happen by worrying about it.

The other aspect of anxiety is what this fear does to the brain and the body—it shuts them down, constricts them, and closes them off. Vital organs aren't getting what they need and the brain is being pushed into fight-or-flight, therefore you're not thinking as clearly. When you're relaxed and thinking clearly, you can often find solutions that evade you when you're upset and worrying. The more you can relax and allow the fear (that isn't helping matters) subside, the better your brain works. Have you ever seen anyone, including yourself, handle a situation effectively and efficiently while freaking out? I haven't. It simply doesn't happen. The more calm we are, the better our brain works. It's that simple.

Challenging situations are an excellent opportunity to work on spirituality and faith. If you've done everything you can do from an action perspective, you simply need to leave the results to a power greater than yourself. There's literally nothing else you can do, so why not use it as an opportunity to grow? I was able to do this in one of the most emotional, fearful situations of my life. When I was going for placement and custody of my son, I realized that I had a lot of anxiety and fear around what would happen if he didn't come to live with me. I needed to put as much positive energy and faith into the Divine as I could while taking whatever action I was capable of, and ultimately leaving the results up to God. I had to take my hands off what I wanted to happen and trust that whatever was in our highest good would happen. I'm very happy to say things went my way and my son moved in with me after the first day. Although it would have hurt, I was prepared to handle it if things went the other way. I would have had to trust that some good was going to come out of it someday.

I had negative experiences in family court previously so to put aside the past and anchor into my faith wasn't easy. As long as I put my so-called faith in the court system—I felt fear. Once I took back the power I was giving away to the courts and put it where it belonged, with my Higher Power, things shifted dramatically.

I mix in these stories of my personal experiences to show you the pages of this book are not theory, they are fact. These things work, I know because I've used them personally. I've also seen countless others use them. This is the beauty of spiritual law—it works every time, all the time, when it's implemented properly.

Chapter 22

Fear from the Past

Regret has no positive benefit or constructive purpose. There is nothing more pointless than wishing the past was different. It's like walking around in sadness and pain, year after year, because you wanted to write something with a blue pen and all you had was a black pen. You can take action today and buy blue pens for the future. You can apologize to someone who asked you to use a blue pen and explain that's all you had at the time, but carrying regret around for years would be ridiculous. Why? Because it doesn't change the reality of the past. Nothing does. Yet we do this constantly in other areas of our lives. We beat ourselves up for something that happened in the past that we cannot change. All we can do is learn from it and do better next time. Feeling bad has no constructive benefits. It lowers our self-esteem and energy levels, thereby making us more incapable of handling future situations well. It directs us toward becoming worse, not better.

Sometimes, I use the analogy of a cheetah hunting a gazelle to explain this. Imagine a cheetah chasing a gazelle. First the gazelle breaks left, then right, and then right again. The cheetah breaks left, then right, and then left, thereby losing its chance at dinner. Now picture the cheetah sulking behind a bush and saying, "I'm the stupidest cheetah on the planet! Gazelles always break left, right, right. I know this! I've seen it a hundred times! But here I am left, right, left...like a fool. I'm probably never going to eat again, I don't even know why I bother. I suck! And I know the others saw this because it was right out in the open. I'm never going to live it down."

It sounds ridiculous picturing an animal behaving this way, but that's what we do to ourselves all the time. We can learn from our past. There's nothing wrong with saying "left, right, right" over and over to get it to sink in. Use the past, learn from it, make amends when necessary, but don't judge yourself for it.

Beating ourselves up reduces energy, self-love, and self-respect. Focusing on it brings on more of the same. It behaves the same way that anxiety does by bringing on what we don't want. The more we think about what we don't want, whether it's in the future or the past, the more energy we're putting toward recreating more of it in the future. Remember, we've been living life backwards from the outside in; the reality is that we live from the inside out. What's happening inside us is reflected in our external experiences. We create the world around us and our experiences. When I was living a life of anger and frustration, I had angry and frustrated people coming at me all the time. People picked fights with me for no apparent reason. Fortunately, I've had that experience only one time in the past 16 years. That one exception was actually an opportunity, given to me by the Universe, to stand in my new Truth and handle things differently so that I could change my physical vibration and transcend that part of my life for good. It is a fond memory and a thoroughly enjoyable experience to know you can handle something in a new way.

We've been conditioned to believe that punishment is the way to change behavior so we incessantly punish ourselves. In psychological studies, they've actually proven that negative reinforcement doesn't change negative behavior, only positive reinforcement does that. We must stop putting ourselves down if we expect to find happiness. Again, we can learn from our past, however, punishing ourselves for it by carrying around negative energy and self-hatred only strips us of the energy necessary to move forward and do better. Make amends when appropriate, learn from your past, and let go of regret—it's the only way to find the joy you're looking for.

We'll dive deeper into this mentality in the next chapter on Acceptance.

Chapter 23

Acceptance

Acceptance plays an important role in our life experience. There are times when we don't like what someone did, how things went, or the circumstances we're in at the moment. Very often, we strongly resist these things. This is why it's been said that all suffering is "resistance to what is." If we resist the fact that someone has transitioned to the "other side," or the fact that our lover has left us for another, or that we don't like our current job, we will experience suffering. If we resist the fact that there is traffic or that we didn't get the laundry done as planned, we'll suffer.

We often confuse suffering as coming from the event itself, when most of the suffering is coming from resistance to the situation. Sure, the situation itself can cause some uncomfortable feelings, but the majority is coming from our resistance.

If we accept the reality of the situation, we can process the emotions in a healthy way, determine what to do next, and move on. Instead, we focus on how wrong it was, how it shouldn't have happened, and how much we don't like that it happened. The reality of the situation is that it happened or is happening, and no amount of complaining or thinking it should be different is going to change that. If it's in the past, labeling it as wrong doesn't change the reality that it happened. If it's happening now, all you need to do is to understand you'd like to head in the direction of something else and look for your next move.

It's like getting stuck in quicksand. If you sit there worrying, complaining, or thrashing around, consumed by the fact that you don't want to be there, it just makes it worse and you continue sinking deeper. If you calm down and accept the situation for what it is, you can get on with the business of getting out. Once you've accepted being in quicksand, you can relax. It will pull your brain out of the fight-or-flight response and allow you to think more clearly and look for solutions. Perhaps you can reach a branch. Is there one behind you? If you lean to the side, can you touch solid ground? How about the other side? Can you use the short stick to pull over the longer stick? Can you whistle for your horse named Trigger to pull you out? The point is, if you stop focusing on the problem and begin focusing on the solution, you will have a much better chance of changing the situation you're in, or not experiencing it again.

Acceptance allows you to let go of the problem and focus on the solution. In the case of accepting past situations, I'll jump to an extreme example to make the point. There's a stigma in society that there is something wrong with death. We get rid of bodies quickly, and then immediately act as if it shouldn't have happened in most situations. This affects us unconsciously. It's common for people to combine an unconscious (or conscious) belief that someone shouldn't have died with the sorrow of missing them. Missing someone can be difficult to work through on its own. When it is combined with a belief that it shouldn't have happened, it's nearly impossible.

If we're capable of understanding that acceptance of the event is more important than our labeling it as bad, we're on our way. Of course we didn't want it to happen, but it did. So, if we can let go of the mental recording playing over and over, saying that "it shouldn't" and "it's not fair," we can get on with the process of healing. There is no universal law that states all Beings will live a certain number of years and if they don't, something went wrong. Yet we often act as if that's the case.

Wishing something didn't happen doesn't make sense. It did happen. It could take years to work through the shock and trauma of the situation, depending on the circumstance, but being focused on thinking something shouldn't have happened blocks that process. You can't work through something until you get to the point of acceptance. Once you accept the reality of the problem, you can begin working on a solution.

This is usually more difficult when younger people pass away because there's a stronger feeling that it shouldn't have happened. I have great compassion for anyone who experiences an emotional and traumatic event, but I'm using this as a teaching tool about acceptance because it's an extreme example. It should be easier to use this process in any situation that is less extreme. And, if someone can use it in a situation like the example, the healing will be profound. There are instances of people succeeding at this. No one is saying you'll ever be "the same" once you experience a traumatic event, but you can heal and experience peace and happiness again.

- Acceptance does not say: I agree that this should have happened and I'm okay that it did.

- Acceptance does say: Even though I wish this didn't happen, I understand and accept the reality that it did.

Knowing there is suffering in not accepting the reality of these situations, can you imagine the suffering that comes from non-acceptance of who and what you are? Much of it is unconscious, but there are deep levels of shame when we think there is something inherently wrong with us. I'll touch on this in the next chapter.

Chapter 24

The Dangers of Shame

Shame is a powerful, low-level vibration, it can induce depression which is another dangerous low-level vibration. I believe Dr. Brené Brown said it best after her in-depth research on courage, vulnerability, shame and guilt. Dr. Brown said guilt is when you feel you *did* something wrong, and shame is when you feel you *are* something wrong. Guilt is bad enough. Feeling we've done something wrong can be extremely detrimental unless we deal with it. However, if we feel that there is something wrong with us, it takes it to a whole different level.

You see, hope diminishes when we feel there is something inherently wrong with us. If we feel there is something wrong with us, it implies we're broken and can't be fixed. There is no hope for a better future or a different outcome because we are defective in some way; and where there is a lack of hope, depression settles in. Depression is dangerous because there is no drive to do things differently. Anger and other low-vibrating energies, such as jealousy, blame, and frustration, can push us to make change. Often it's in unhealthy ways, however they do attempt to induce movement which can change the situation. But depression just gives up and that is more dangerous. This is why shame and depression so often walk hand in hand.

So, what can we do when we notice shame within us? Go into it. We must face it and get outside help. Not necessarily professional help, although that's usually recommended, but you will need some sort of help. Shame breeds in silence. We need to open up and discuss it. When it's hidden, it's shame. Shame doesn't survive the light, so bring it to the light and work through it.

I'm going to refer to my favorite quote from ACIM for this one: "Nothing real can be threatened. Nothing unreal exists. Herein lies the peace of God." At your core you are eternal, real, perfect, and divine. You cannot be threatened. Nothing you did or experienced can damage you. Your mind-made self and your temporary emotional/mental state can be damaged. However, since they can be threatened, they're not actually "real" in an eternal sense because they don't technically exist on a soul level. As you identify with the True You and disidentify with the mind-made you, herein lies the peace of God.

We all experience shame at one time or another, but when it's our own shame, each of us feels like our situation is different. We feel that way because otherwise, it wouldn't be shame. Our shame is on a different, deeper level that others wouldn't understand, and they would never look at us the same if they knew about it. It's an amazing feeling when shame is shared with someone who is trustworthy. When a safe space of non-judgment is present, shame cannot live or thrive in that space. It dissipates and becomes easier to transcend. It may take some courage, but it's so worth it! There is only so much happiness and peace we can experience when we walk around with shame inside. At some point, dealing with it is necessary to the expansion and growth you're trying to achieve. Find a safe person to help you walk through this—you won't regret it!

PART 4

THE SPIRITUAL LIFE

Chapter 25

Follow the Nudges

If we're going to move forward in our growth, it's important to learn to follow the nudges. The nudge is what you followed when you picked up this book—it's another name for intuition. People would like to be in tune with their intuition but tend to go about it the wrong way. It's often overlooked and ignored, then searched for with great intensity and panic. On one hand, we ignore it when it comes. On the other, when we decide we want it, we put so much effort into trying to make the intuition appear that we unknowingly stuff it down even further through the contraction of our effort and control.

You will notice in this book and other spiritual texts that spiritual terms carry a certain energy. There's a certain style and feel to them. Here is a list of spiritual terms and their counterparts to highlight the contrast between the two:

> **Spiritual terms**: allow, forget, remember, relax, loosen, silence, peace, contentment, stillness, listen, non-resistance, open.

> **Non-spiritual terms**: make happen, try, push, effort, figure out, think, control, contract, tighten, constrict, noise, frustration, busyness, resistance, close.

Spiritual terms are non-action words while non-spiritual terms imply action. The words "open" and "close" are very telling and get right to the heart of what I'm explaining.

We have two options: One is to open, and the other is to close. If we open, life flows through us. We can remember the Truth of who we are, we can forget what society has taught us that no longer serves us, and we can be pliable and go with the flow while experiencing the peace and contentment that comes with non-resistance.

If we choose to close, we tighten up and the life force is limited. We push and try to make things happen, attempting to figure out what's going to happen next and how to control it. All the while, we are caught up in the noise and frustration of not being able to hear the nudges because we're too constricted to allow them to naturally bubble up.

To hear and follow the nudges, we need to integrate the spiritual terms into our lives the best we can. This is counterintuitive to the way society has taught us, and quite frankly it's how the external world works, so it's a big adjustment. The Temporal Realm is linear: You do this, then this, and then you get that. You go to work, do your job, and then get a paycheck. With spirituality, things aren't linear; it just always is. Have you ever asked, "Who sings that song? You know the one, about the thing that's kinda like what we were just talking about…you know, the song? Oh never mind, I'll stop thinking about it and it'll come to me." Then five minutes later, you remember the artist *and* the song title.

The reason this works is because we're not "trying" to remember. We're not "forcing it," so it naturally arises within us without the effort. When we push and try to remember, it doesn't work. We need to interact with our spiritual selves through allowing and non-action instead of "trying" to make something happen. Too much effort constricts the very flow of what naturally comes from within.

As we begin to live by following the nudges, we can ask for assistance. Ask your Source for your awareness to be heightened around a certain situation. This is one of my favorite prayers. It's based on the mentality of a commonly held Truth: *God will not do for us what we can do for ourselves.* There is Truth to this. We are co-creators and need to take responsibility for the direction of our own lives and participate. That being said, there's another side to this coin that's rarely examined: God *will* do for us what we cannot do for ourselves. This is wonderful news! This means that if we can't do something, God will help us. How can we change something if we're unaware of it? We can't. Therefore, asking for *awareness* for something you'd like to change works tremendously well!

"Please God, help me be aware of your nudges. Please let them capture my attention in a way so that I don't simply shrug them off. Please let me notice them and have the strength to act on them."

Once you set this intention, be prepared to do your part. When the nudge captures your attention, it's your responsibility to not dismiss it or think you're too busy to pay attention to it. You must stop for a moment and give the nudge your attention. See what it's saying, write it down for later, or make a note in your phone. Do whatever you need to do, but pay attention. Take it seriously and hold it with reverence. You see, what we focus on expands. Focus on your nudges when they do come and when they do capture your attention. By doing so, they'll come more often, you'll become more familiar with them, and you'll be able to implement them into your life in more ways.

After learning to recognize the nudges, it's a matter of following through on them. Start with something small and see it through so you can gain confidence in it. You used your nudge system to obtain this book, and now this book is explaining how to recognize it and use it better. Now that's a nudge! Pay attention to it, follow it, allow it, play around with it, and watch it develop into the practical navigation tool it was meant to be.

Chapter 26

God Loves Us and Wants Us to Succeed

I'd like to take a giant leap backwards to gain some big-picture perspective on how things work and how simple it is to see the Truth of things. To take this leap, we need to agree on one thing:

> *There is something that has a level of Divine wisdom*
> *and intelligence which created everything and that it is*
> *based in Love and/or its own self-expansion.*

If we can agree on that, we're good. If you can attempt to look at things through that window to see if it might possibly hold water, we're good.

Whether there is a God who is personal to us that loves us, or there is a Universe that is simply interested in its own expansion and we are part of that Universe, it really doesn't matter for what I am teaching you. It all comes out the same way. You can determine what you choose to believe for yourself.

With this mindset, would you smash your toe with a hammer for no apparent reason? Of course not. You wouldn't intentionally hurt a part of you. If your leg were broken and you couldn't walk, would you attempt to fix it? Would you get it set so it could heal and be mobile again? Of course you would. It's part of you. If it works better and is more functional, then you work better and are more functional.

If you believe in a Loving Creator that wants what's best for you out of sheer love, the same things apply. Innately we love our creations, so would we purposely hurt one of our creations for no reason? No, of course not. Would we support our creations in becoming happier, more full versions of themselves? Yes, of course we would.

From this line of logic, I'll take that giant step backwards and share the perspective that if you can't picture a Loving Creator saying it to you, then it probably isn't true. Assume there's a Universe in the process of expanding and therefore supporting our expansion, would it support what you are doing?

From here, through either perspective, I can determine that if I am working toward the expansion of myself, I have the force of the entire Universe and/or the Loving God itself supporting me in full. That doesn't suck! I mean, really! Look at the implications. The omnipresent, omniscient, and omnipotent creative forces of the Universe are supporting you in whatever you do to become a happier, fuller version of yourself. The Creative Intelligence that designed and maintains the entire Universe, the galaxies within it, the migrations of animals all over the world, the countless babies growing within other creations, all while keeping planets at the proper distances, etc. is behind you 100 percent! If the Universe or God can do all these things synchronistically, it can certainly find you a job, an apartment, or a spouse. It's an easy task, if we're open to allowing it to flow through us.

It behooves the Universe to help you simply because if it helps you, it helps itself, not to mention the whole love thing!

Think of what you can accomplish with the Powers That Be at your back. The possibilities are endless. Now, life starts looking like the exciting adventure it's supposed to be!

Chapter 27

Building a Wall of Faith

Faith is very useful as you're walking this path. There are many opinions about faith. When someone doesn't have faith, they tend to think the people that have it are "lucky;" like it magically turned up inside of them one day or perhaps they were born with it. Of course, we are born into this world knowing the Truth so we do have some faith coming in...everyone does. We have faith that there will be air to breathe, and that someone will take care of us since we can't take care of ourselves, etc.

Similarly, we're all walking around living by faith without knowing it—even those who consider themselves absent of faith. We have faith that the car will start, the lights will come on when we flip the switch, the car will move, etc. Faith is all around us and we use it all the time. It's not something elusive that only certain people are fortunate enough to have.

Let's take the mystery out of faith to gain clarity. Faith is trusting that if you do one thing, a specific sequential result will follow. The definition of faith is "complete trust or confidence in someone or something." We have complete confidence that if we press the gas pedal, the car will go faster. We have complete trust that our spouse will return home from work (if we're in a healthy relationship). If something we put our faith in doesn't happen, we're surprised or even shocked. This is because we trust that it will happen.

So how are these examples of faith developed? At one point, you didn't have faith in these things. Over time, you developed it. You learned to trust through repetition and through risk and reward. You flipped the light switch and the light went on. After doing this several times, you developed faith that it would continue to work every time you flipped the switch. Now, you don't even think about it anymore. This is true faith.

Spiritual faith works the same way—it develops through repetition. I'm not asking you to blindly believe in anything. I'm asking you to try it and, if it works, begin to trust that it will continue to work. Some people say we shouldn't test God. God doesn't have an ego and doesn't get offended by us, we're not going to hurt God's feelings because our Creator loves us unconditionally. And for those who believe in an impersonal Universe, it's the same deal: the Universe has no ego. It's not going to throw a bunch of wrathful energy around because a part of it was trying to figure out how its laws work. You're good, no worries.

So, how do you build faith? You experiment with it and try it out. Begin by handing something small over that has minimal consequences. You could begin with something that you can't do anything about anyway, something that's out of your hands. Let's say you've studied for a test to the best of your ability, or you've prepared for a meeting or an event to the best of your ability, but you're still worried about how it's going to turn out. You can say something like: "Okay God, I'm handing the results of this over to you. I've done everything I can on my end and it's too late to do anything more now. I'm going to hand the results over to you. I'm trying to build my faith, so I'm taking my hands off something that I have no control over and giving it to you. I'm going to trust that after is all said and done, it will turn out to be in my highest good. I won't judge too quickly. I'll give it a little time to see how it affects my life for the better, even if it doesn't go how I want, because I know sometimes unanswered prayers turn out to be the greatest blessings. I am handing this over to you to build faith that you will help me and that things are happening *for* me, not *to* me." Then let go of the worry and see how it plays out.

If you've been working on yourself in any way, you should be able to look back over your life and see many instances where things have happened *for* you. Where synchronicities happened in your favor, where you were kept safe or taken care of by whatever force you believe in. Whether you're handing things over now or looking back on your past for examples, everything you've experienced for your good can be used as building blocks of faith. Picture building a brick wall and that every little experience that worked out for you is a brick. When that truck blew through a red light and missed you by a split second, that's a brick. When your boyfriend or girlfriend broke up with you and you prayed for them to come back, only to find a new level of happiness without them, that's a big, old cinder block. (Big things get cinder blocks). When your child got lost in a crowded place and sheer terror shot through you for a moment, only to find them a moment later, that's a brick. When you were feeling depressed and couldn't see any way that things could get better, but somehow they did, that's a cinder block. Pay attention to all the good that has happened in your life and build your wall of faith. Hold these things dearly and don't dismiss them as coincidences. Internalize them, make them part of you and your wall of faith. That's how faith is built…it's developed over time and experiences. It's the same as trust; it needs to be earned. Trust me when I say that if you look close enough, you'll realize it's already been earned. But feel free to keep testing and building, a bigger faith wall is a better faith wall!

The beauty of this wall is two-fold: Not only does it forever grow if you put your attention on it, but you can also use it at any time. You don't have to wait until it's done. Occasionally in life, a situation will arise when you need to lean on your wall of faith. Maybe you're in one of those situations now. That's when you lean on your wall. It can sound like this: "God, I'm scared, this is a big one. I don't know if I have the faith for this. It's bigger than anything I've faced before. I'm going to look back on my bricks and blocks in the hope that as I remind myself of all the times you've been there and kept me safe, I will be able to lean on that and trust you to get me through this in one piece."

Start going over all your bricks and every single block, taking a moment to feel the support as you remember each one. Let your heart be filled with love as you mull over a cinder block that you thought was going to take you down for sure, but it turned out to be one of your largest blessings. Allow yourself to feel the support that has always been there when you've opened to it. Feel the gratitude that comes with the recognition of being fully supported by something as great and wonderful as the Creative Energy that flows through all. Trust that Love. Have faith in that presence. Lean on your wall.

This practice has worked for me through many small and large situations over the years. Now, if something tries to shake my faith, I laugh at it. A little spiritual laugh that comes when you are conscious of the Truth and how silly it is when our humanness begins to worry about inconsequential things.

Chapter 28

Spiritual Laughter

Laughter is not only the best medicine, it can be a great spiritual practice and a sign that you're heading in the right direction or finally realizing the Truth about something. When we see things clearly, they become laughable.

One example, if someone had three months to live and you told them their cable bill was a week late, they would probably laugh. Most of the things that we stress over are downright silly, and when we see them for what they really are, the natural reaction is laughter.

This often happens with my clients when we're discussing serious topics. As we dissect what they're worried about, they will literally break out laughing because most of it is so absurd that we have to laugh. The beauty is that when you're seeing the Truth, you can sense there is no blame or negative feelings. You simply didn't know what you didn't know when you didn't know it. Now that you know, you'll do better. It's as simple as that.

While writing this book, several things appeared in my life that needed to be handled at the same time. There were times I had so many things to do, fear would try to grip me. Fear would attempt to tell me that I'd never get it all done or that hitting a deadline was of paramount importance. As I leaned away from that fear and saw things the way they actually were, I would laugh. I'd laugh at the attempts of fear to overtake me. Laugh at the implication that if I didn't get something done by a certain time, my life would suffer dramatically. It's silly. If my book didn't come out when I planned, it would come out later—that's okay. It's not that important what day my book comes out. My ego wants to tell me that it does matter and I have to push forward while stressing out over things like this. But that's not the Truth. The Truth is that even though this is a large, exciting project, it simply doesn't matter when it comes out. It'll come out when the time is right. Thinking anything other than that causes stress, makes the task harder, and is literally laughable when you really look at it.

There's no judgement for my brain attempting to talk me into something untrue. It was simply pointing out the possibility of an experience I might not enjoy—missing a deadline. It was up to me to take that information and determine whether I should take action, feel stress, give up, or simply laugh at it. There's also no judgement towards myself if I had leaned into the fear, got caught up in it for a while, and then recognized the futility of what had grabbed a hold of me. As I recognize the Truth in a spiritual way, I simply giggle and see it for the True silliness that my humanness can cause at times. I'm joyful and grateful that I see it for what it is now and I'm no longer in its grips.

So, when the laughter comes on your spiritual path, take notice because you're probably seeing something very truthful for the first time. Even in comedy, the funniest things have some truth to them. One of my favorite ways to grow is through laughter. It certainly beats being curled up in a ball crying and wailing for two hours, although that can be helpful at times as well.

Take a long, serious look at some of the things that bother you. Follow your line of thinking down to the core. Keep asking "what" and "why." Or "what does this mean?" Follow it all the way down to the core of the Truth and see if there's laughter there. If you find the laughter, you've found the Truth!

Chapter 29

Prayer or Scared-Talking?

To wrap up the faith discussion, I'll discuss prayer. You can worry or pray, but you can't do both at the same time. This statement cuts through a lot of the misunderstandings about prayer. Many times, people pray about an issue, asking for help from the Universe, God, the Creator, the Divine or a Power greater than them. After the prayer, they continue worrying about the issue as if this all-powerful force can't handle the job. Like most things, you need to slow down and think things through before you see the Truth.

Let's put this through the logic detector. If you've just asked for help from an omni-loving, omni-powerful, and omni-present Source that is the Wisdom that designed and keeps the Universe functioning in complete and immutable law, do you think it might be able to find you a job? I'd say it could probably handle the task. Yet, worry abounds because faith is lacking.

For example, we often put more faith in an online order than we do in God. We put in the order and forget about it, expecting our package to show up at the door in a few days. In fact, we have so much faith, we usually forget it's coming and get excited to find a surprise for us on the doorstep. When we show more faith in an online, man-made delivery system that has possible flaws than we do in the Creator of the Universe—there's a problem. If you'd like to experience the safety, comfort, and joy your Creator has in store for you, you must begin to develop a relationship of trust with it.

Faith is strengthened through it's conscious use. You can expand your faith by using it to the best of your ability. If you pray for help, you will receive help. However, you can't receive the help if you don't believe it's going to happen. That's not faith; that's just "scared-talking."

I know this isn't easy and fortunately, so does the Creator. That's why perfection is not a requirement; it's simply the faith of a small child or the faith of a mustard seed is all that's needed. The system doesn't work based on the quality of the process. It works off the earnest desire to connect and have a relationship based in Love. If you earnestly seek, you will find. Knock and the door will open. Shall I continue with the references?

You get the point. If there's something we would like to have in our lives, we must put energy towards it—this includes a relationship with our Creator. Whenever possible, begin with something small then pray, hand it over and let it go. Assume it is done and it shall be. Build your relationship of trust, your wall of faith, and enjoy the peace that comes with it. Of course we need to be careful what we ask for because it cannot be detrimental to others. It also may be fulfilled in a way that we didn't expect. But if we ask, we shall receive. All we have to do is let go and believe. Practice believing and begin receiving.

Chapter 30

Back-Door Intention Setting

I'm a firm believer in finding and doing what works. There is a great way to approach things that can outwit your conditioned patterns. I call it *coming in the back door*. Instead of trying to override deeply conditioned patterns by coming in the front door, let's go around the back and avoid the patterns all together. We can even use other conditioned behaviors to support us in this clever tactic. Here are two examples to illustrate.

In the first example, you may be unsure of what to do in a situation. The front door says that you need to do whatever you can to find the right answer. Sometimes, the decision is difficult or there are multiple possibilities. We simply don't have the perspective to see into the future and know which is the right decision. So, we can look for the back door. First get still and say, "God, I've done what I can to come to the correct conclusion here, but I'm not sure I'm making the right decision. If this is the wrong decision and it isn't in my highest good, please shut the door on this possibility before I continue. If nothing stops me from choosing this answer, I'm going ahead with it on Monday. If this isn't the right thing, please shut the door on it before Monday. Thank you."

Then, trust. Know that your Creator has a much better vantage point than you do, so leave it in those hands instead of yours. This method has worked wonderfully for me in many situations including this one. I decided to rent a home for my son and myself. After I said this prayer, the owners informed me they were selling and wouldn't be renting to me. So I ended up finding a more desirable place on a seven-acre horse farm and enjoyed living in a much better atmosphere with benefits I never could have anticipated.

This is also a great technique when learning to receive. Learning to receive in a healthy way can be difficult for people on the spiritual path. They are such strong givers that they're out of balance with receiving. The front door implies that you need to go against your conditioning that tells you receiving is selfish. That is a deeply embedded belief system that can take some time to work through. So, let's check the back door. The back door says that if you understand the process of giving and receiving better, you'd be selfish not to receive. Let's look at this closer.

Everything is cyclical. It's in breath, out breath…give, receive…full circle. This is how things continue, by feeding themselves. If things were one-sided, they'd burn out. Since giving and receiving is a full circle, you need to do both. This is a good start, but the real back door is that it feels good to give. You're a giver. If you don't allow someone to give to you, you're blocking them from feeling the joy of giving, as well as completing their cycle so it can continue. They just want to experience the joy that you experience. Instead, you're standing in their way and saying, "No, I won't allow you to feel good. Only I get to feel good by giving." Pure selfishness.

Let's take this one step further and see what It says to the other person, as well as ourselves. The energy and the unconscious messages that this sends to others and that we internalize ourselves is very damaging.

> **To the other person, it says**: "I don't want what you're trying to give me. It's not good enough for me. I don't want to accept the kindness you're attempting to direct toward me."

> **To you, it says**: "I don't deserve this gift. I'm not important or special enough to have people give to me. I'm not worthy of receiving."

By coming in the back door, you need to understand that you're helping others feel good. It's selfish *not* to receive. By allowing them to give, you can break through all the conditioned patterns telling you "no". It's much easier coming in this door than the front. These

94

are two examples of a process that outwits the psyche and makes spiritual progress more fluid and easier to attain.

PART 5

DEEP TRUTHS

Chapter 31

Love and Fear

Another core understanding is the fundamental nature of our experiences here on earth. When we get there, we find that all our emotions are based on love and fear.

What is fear? Fear is the energy that all negative emotions are based in. Anger, sadness, jealousy, frustration, etc., are all versions of fear. When our sense of security is threatened, fear arises and manifests in many different ways; it can show itself by undermining our sense of well-being, our relationships, even in our financial security.

One of the hardest times to see this is when someone is lashing out in anger. On the surface, it seems they're inflicting negativity onto someone else, which they are. However, underneath, they are scared of something and the only way they know how to deal with that fear is to project anger onto someone else. To make them feel the way they feel—like a victim of something. Looking closely at anger lets us see that it isn't a form of strength, it's actually a form of weakness coming from a place of fear. A behavior that's triggered when someone is unable to feel safe in their environment or situation.

On the flip side, Love is at the core of all positive emotions. Happiness, excitement, contentment, joy, and romance are all based in love. When we experience a positive feeling, it is a version of love. Of course, some may be stronger versions than others, such as liking a car or loving your spouse. One example is contentment. Oftentimes people don't associate contentment with love; but if you look closely, you can see that when you're experiencing contentment, it's usually because you have love for what you're experiencing and/or the person you're with. Being able to sit in a room with someone without saying or doing anything and feeling "content" is often a sign of love in that relationship.

Now, we'll take this a step deeper. Technically, there is no such "thing" as fear. Whaaaaaaat? That's right, fear is not real. Fear is merely the absence of love.

Let's use lightness and darkness to explain this because it's often used in reference to love and fear. When a room is dark, there isn't a "thing" called "darkness" in it that we need to usher out; it's just absence of light. When we walk in with a flashlight, there is no struggle between darkness and light. There simply is light there now and the darkness is gone. It's the same thing with fear. When there's fear, it's just absence of love. When we bring in love, there's no struggle; the fear is just gone. Love is there now.

The most profound Truths are always simple. Take a moment, wrap your brain around it, and then attempt to implement it in a real-life situation. Think of a situation where you're feeling negative (nothing too intense yet, this is your first try), perhaps getting cut off in traffic and barely avoiding an accident. Initially you may feel anger, then trace the feeling down to your fear. For example, you had a fear of wrecking your vehicle or getting physically hurt. Once you've identified your fear, you can introduce love and feel gratitude for your safety and compassion for other people's mistakes. We all get distracted at times or make poor choices in the heat of the moment. Start imagining love coming into the situation that's causing the fear, and you'll feel a sense of peace begin to arise. Depending on the situation you're using this with, you may not be able to see how to fix the situation (if it needs to be fixed). However, you can experience a new calmness and you'll be able to think more clearly while looking for a solution. Most situations don't even need to be "fixed," so bringing love in can dissipate the fear and you can move on filled with love.

Next time you're experiencing a negative emotion like anger or frustration, recognize it as a version of fear and then bring in love. Can you imagine if many of us did this as often as possible? What a wonderful world it will be!

Chapter 32

Strength through Vulnerability

As we walk through this experiential life, there are things capable of knocking us around on a regular basis if we're not stable within ourselves. The healing that we need to do from the unconscious experiences we've had up until now can also be extremely difficult. There is an inner strength we all have and need to lean on in times of difficulty. This is what is often referred to as the Spiritual Warrior. When I first heard the term, I liked it. It sounded powerful and really "bad ass," which my ego liked. As I ceased fighting things, the term Spiritual Warrior began to lose its luster. I didn't want to be a warrior of any kind. I didn't want to fight things. I'd been fighting things all my life and I was tired. I had surrendered the fight and found so much freedom in the surrender that the last thing I wanted to do was to start fighting again. Besides, I couldn't picture a Loving God saying, "Glenn, go out into battle and fight against things. That's what you must do in life. Fight!" It didn't feel right or make sense, so I simply dropped the term from my vocabulary.

After a while of being consistent with my spiritual disciplines, I began seeing the term more regularly. One day, it caught my attention and I stopped. I thought, why do I keep seeing this? Why do spiritual people I resonate with use it? Is there something I'm missing? Is there another way to see it? I asked myself, "What traits does a warrior have?" I immediately came up with courage...ooh, I like courage! That's a word that resonates and feels powerful, but doesn't imply fighting anything or anyone. I definitely like it! This is when I embraced the term in a new way.

A Spiritual Warrior isn't about attacking or violence; it's about courage. It's not about the absence of fear; it's about standing firm in the presence of fear and thereby transcending it. A Spiritual Warrior stands firm in its beliefs, doesn't sway, and does what is necessary even though fear is present. With these traits, a Spiritual Warrior is capable of Being who they truly are and healing what is necessary to heal. How courageous!

In this world, there's a major imbalance of energies. We instinctively identify with the masculine aspect of things and don't stop to look at the feminine aspect. Of course, this can be even more out of balance in men because the masculine energy is usually stronger and society's teachings reinforce that mindset. I'll get into the feminine and masculine energies more, but for now let's focus on true strength and what that looks like.

The mentality of the Spiritual Warrior steers us in the direction of where true strength lies: in vulnerability. In my opinion Dr. Brene' Brown has done some amazing research and work, so you'll see occasional references to her teachings. Most people believe that vulnerability is opening yourself up to the possibility of being hurt. Actually, it is opening up and finding out you can't be hurt. This also doubles back to my favorite quote from ACIM: "Nothing real can be threatened. Nothing unreal exists. Herein lies the peace of God."

We are "real," we are eternal and we cannot be threatened. Therefore, opening up doesn't put us at risk of being hurt because we cannot be hurt. This understanding is where true strength comes from.

The only aspect of us that can be hurt in any way is the part that is not real: our temporary self; our mind-made self; our ego. This is who we think we are, who we think we're supposed to be. If we identify with this part of ourselves as who we truly are, we suffer. We must identify with our True Self, the eternal, spiritual center as who we are, while understanding that our egoic identity is simply made up of different roles we play at varying times in our lives. Some of these roles include parent, child, employee, employer, friend, and spouse. These are roles we play, they are not who we really are at our core.

So, if we open up to being vulnerable and someone takes a shot at our ego, we don't have to protect it, we don't have to build a wall around it. We simply need to understand that it isn't us they are attacking. They are attacking the very thing we're trying to disidentify with anyway. No need to defend something we're not identified with. They can have their opinions and we can have ours, but it's not an attack on "you."

The reason true strength is found in vulnerability comes from the fundamental Truth of opening and closing. We always have a choice in every situation to either open or close, allow or constrict. Closing is never the answer if we expect to have peace, and opening always is the answer. We can never build a defensive wall tall enough or wide enough for it to be impenetrable. Eventually something always finds a way to hurt us because of the endlessly changing circumstances of life. This is also what it means to build our own prison. In the process of protecting ourselves from being hurt, we build a stronger and stronger prison, keeping ourselves inside and minimizing contact with the outside world in an attempt to prevent pain. If we get good enough at building walls, our lives have minimal experiences and therefore minimal joy.

The egoic things we're attempting to protect are simply triggers from events earlier in life that bring up emotional pain trapped within us. Once we close off and stuff the pain from an experience, it remains inside until it's activated again by a similar situation. If we stop trying to protect our triggers from being touched and allow healing to occur when they are touched, they will cease being our triggers. If we can begin seeing emotional pain arising as an opportunity to heal and become more of ourselves, we can learn to embrace it. If we open when we feel triggered and allow the pain to flow out, instead of closing and locking it in by trying to avoid it, we can transcend it.

In actuality, most of the pain we feel is our resistance to what's happening, not pain from the situation itself. If we open to the pain, we'll find that it's much easier to deal with than we anticipated. Letting go of the thought that this shouldn't be happening, or that there's something wrong with the fact that it happened dramatically reduces the suffering and leaves you with a surmountable amount of pain. Don't ask, "Why is this happening to me?" Ask a more empowering question, like "How can I use this to open up and become more of who I want to be?"

We must open to the Truth of who and what we are and identify with the eternal aspect of ourselves that can't be threatened. Only here can we be safe and unharmed. Only through vulnerability and openness can we dance with life and all its experiences in joyful ecstasy and utter safety. Embrace your birthright and your destiny.

Chapter 33

Authenticity

One of the reasons we feel hurt when our ego is attacked is because of our innate desire to connect with others. This is innate because we all have it and it serves a purpose. The desire to connect helps us form families and communities, so we can lean on each other's strengths to achieve and experience that which we could never do alone. We fundamentally need each other to thrive. It also serves as a motivation to procreate and expand our species.

The problem arises when we over identify with the ego as who we are. When we experience what we perceive to be rejection, it hurts tremendously. What we need to understand is that no one is rejecting "us," they are rejecting the "representation of us" we decided to show them. The egoic self of who-we-think-we-should-be is meeting their egoic self of who-they-think-they-should-be. Their representative is meeting our representative. This is superficial at best.

When we authentically share who we truly are, we are rarely rejected because the other person senses our authenticity. Even if they did reject us, it wouldn't hurt because our authentic self cannot be hurt by someone else's ego. Our True Self would recognize the ego in the other person immediately and wouldn't take it personally. There would be no reason to take it personally. This is why it's impossible to argue with someone who is completely present. When someone is connected to who they truly are, there's no reason to be defensive because they can't be hurt. There is space for the other person to have their opinions and lash out without it affecting them. They are completely open, vulnerable, and can stand unflinchingly in the light and courage of the Spiritual Warrior.

There's also no possibility of being rejected by someone standing in their authentic self. If someone is connected to the Truth authentically, they have the awareness that we are all one. Therefore, how could they reject anyone? It would be the same as rejecting themselves.

As we learn to stand in the authenticity of who we are, there is less separation and more inclusiveness. We are more alike than we are different and being authentic helps us see this. We all want peace, love, connection, and to be accepted for who we are. True connection happens when we get underneath all our differences and meet each other at the core.

This is also the best place to meet to resolve conflict—on common ground. Begin where there is agreement and work backwards from there. It's helpful to understand others when the framework is connection, not separation. Once you find that both sides want peace and happiness as opposed to being "right," solutions can be found.

As you can see, being authentic has many benefits, I'll touch on one more before moving on—self-love. How do we expect to love ourselves if we don't allow our True selves to be seen? Unconsciously that says: there's something wrong with me, so I have to present something other than myself to be accepted by others. How do we expect to have self-love if the very way we interact on a daily basis derives from denial of Self? We simply can't. Self-acceptance and self-love are the foundation for receiving acceptance and love from others. We have to be real with ourselves first and then we can be real with others.

Chapter 34

Feminine/Masculine Energies

The world has been dramatically out of balance energy-wise for thousands of years. We can see this in the way women have been treated, as well as how masculine energy has dominated causing so many problems throughout the ages.

There have been societies that understood and embraced the strength of the Divine Feminine but they are rare in history. The aggressiveness of unconscious behavior has been the dominant vibration since the beginning. Violence and greed have been primary resulting in the world we have today. This is why the spiritual shift is happening now—we can't continue on this way. We must come into balance with both masculine and feminine energies while reconnecting to Source if we are to survive as a species. To wrap our brains around the two types of energies, here is a list showing the differences.

Masculine Energy	vs	Feminine Energy [2]
Doing	vs	Being
Aggression	vs	Surrender
Analytical	vs	Intuitive
Concrete	vs	Abstract

---

[2] http://www.fromthestars.com/page128.html

Impatient	vs	Patient
Movement	vs	Stillness
Striving	vs	Tranquil
Rushing	vs	Nurturing
Assertive	vs	Receptive
Left brain	vs	Right brain
Thrusting	vs	Receiving
Organization	vs	Synthesizing
Logical	vs	Creative
Busy	vs	Calm
Hard	vs	Soft
Controlling	vs	Allowing
Individuality	vs	Unity
Expression	vs	Silence
Constructive	vs	Instructive
Strength	vs	Endurance
Knowledge	vs	Mystery

As you look at the traits, you can see how a lot of the issues that have permeated our societies for millennia have stemmed from a disproportionate amount of masculine energy. Aggression, striving, and logic have ruled, while surrender, tranquility, and creativity have been diminished. There simply is no balance between the energies. Not only has this caused many historic problems, but it is still a major problem in the world today. So what's the solution? More feminine energy, of course.

The beautiful thing about nature is that it always gives us what we need to survive and thrive, if we'll only open to it. Feminine energy is much stronger than masculine energy, simply because it needs to be in order to come into balance. The world is craving feminine energy just as it craves balance. When we identify and embrace our feminine energies, our circumstances improve; they must, to help us move towards balance. If you worked all the time and didn't have any time to recuperate, you'd feel better if you went on vacation. If you were unemployed, sitting around and doing nothing for a long period of time and then began working at a job you enjoyed, you'd feel better. There is a natural, positive reaction to getting into a balanced state that benefits us.

There is so much conflict because of aggression and control in the world that when we bring in surrender and allowing, it diminishes on a large scale. In fact, this is the only way that large-scale social change has taken place. Leaders who have used this to effect massive change in the world are Nelson Mandela, Martin Luther King Jr., and Mahatma Gandhi. Think about how they acted and what they stood for...it was all feminine energy and that's why it worked.

Nelson Mandela stopped responding aggressively and began to be patient and calm. This opened the space for conversations about both side's fears and desires with his perceived enemy. Turning to creativity, they worked together toward a common solution instead of being assertively aggressive to control an outcome.

Martin Luther King Jr. epitomized feminine energy by raising awareness of the detrimental masculine energy in charge (oppression and violence) and inviting feminine energy in the way of nonviolence to be embraced.

Mahatma Gandhi helped free an entire country by stressing passive resistance, nonviolent disobedience, and boycotts. These are all examples of feminine energy. They are non-action as opposed to action oriented.

You see, the only thing that works is feminine energy which looks very similar to the list of "spiritual terms" I mentioned earlier in this book. For a visual reference of the energies, picture a large rock in the middle of a stream. The rock represents masculine energy standing up against the water as if to say, "I am solid, strong, and you shall not pass." The water is the feminine energy that doesn't argue or fight; it simply goes around the rock and continues its path undeterred. Not only does the water win in the short term by getting to where it's going, it also wins in the long term through erosion. Eventually, the rock is worn down and is no longer large enough to attempt resistance. This is how powerful feminine energy is if we decide to embrace it.

You can see feminine energy in the section on setting boundaries. Setting a healthy boundary doesn't force anyone to do anything; it simply allows them to choose which direction the situation will go. Look closely and you'll see feminine energy at work in many places that are healthy and functioning well.

Unfortunately, masculine energy is what people lean towards when they want to change things, even though it doesn't work in the long-term. In psychological studies, negative reinforcement by way of punishment has been proven ineffective in changing people's behaviors. The only thing proven to change behaviors has been positive reinforcement. And yet punishment, an example of masculine control, is still the primary consequence society uses. You can see this in both prisons and parenting.

As a rule, when the topic of strength is mentioned, the mind automatically thinks of masculine strength. Masculine strength is the cause of, and therefore perpetuates, the original problem. We are so delusional that we declare war in the name of achieving peace. You cannot fight for peace. You cannot throw negative, masculine energy at a wall and somehow end up with loving, feminine energy. As Albert Einstein said, "You cannot solve a problem with the consciousness that created it." When we experience something we don't like or strive for something we want, we respond with masculine energy because this has been our only example of strength for so long. Men and women alike lean into this energy. When men do it, it looks more natural because they've been doing it longer. When women do it, it stands out because women have been held down for so long. This is why women who embrace the masculine energies in the business world are labeled negatively. People aren't as conditioned to see aggression or dominance from a woman.

Regardless of your gender, if you're looking for what will work in business or any other area of the world, look to embracing the feminine. The way of patience, intuition, nurturing, and creativity are highly effective, needed, and in demand by society and the world which are both trying to come back into balance. We're literally functioning with only half our skill sets and wondering why things are out of whack. Balance, dear ones, balance.

Chapter 35

Spiritual Law Works Always, Every Time

The beauty of spiritual law is that it works every time, all the time. Once you learn spiritual law and how it operates, you can solve any problem that arises. You can work through anything and make the right move all the time. While there is an enormous spiritual awakening occurring, there is also a large amount of conflict in the world. I believe the conflict, from a broader perspective, can be seen in contrast. What does contrast do? It helps us see things more distinctly, more clearly.

In the world of duality, bilateral reality, yin and yang, there are only two ways to go: love or fear, open or close, positive or negative, external or internal, masculine or feminine, etc. This can simplify life dramatically when learning to navigate it in a healthier, happier, and more fulfilling way. When looking at the reasoning behind decisions you've made or paths you've taken, what have you used to make your determinations?

I'll share some of my personal experiences…

I used to believe that to be successful, I needed to conform to society's expectations. I resisted it consistently for many years (this was fear-based). Once I woke up, I realized that I didn't need to be what society wanted me to be. I needed to let go of the fear and open to who I truly am (this is love-based). Once I did, I found that happiness, fulfillment, and success came my way.

I used to think I'd find happiness if I made good money, bought a house, got married, and had a child. I did all those things and found myself even more unhappy than when I was living as an active alcoholic. While living a dysfunctional life, I basically expected to be unhappy. I felt that life was unfair and I fought against it every step of the way. However, once I followed society's rules for happiness and found out there was no happiness there either, I was really in trouble! Now what? I knew how to pick myself back up after failure, but how do I do that after success? This was the beginning of the end for me. If there's no happiness in failure and no happiness in success—why bother continuing to try? This sent me on a two-year downward spiral until I woke up of course.

While living as an active alcoholic, I avoided my feelings, I rationalized why things weren't my fault, and I blamed my inside state on my external circumstances. When I pulled myself together and acquired all the external things, I again tried basing my internal state on my external circumstances. Neither of these worked. It wasn't until I turned inside and straightened out my internal state that I found the happiness and fulfillment I was longing for. Only then did my external life begin to reflect the fulfillment and happiness I was experiencing on the inside, and only then did my external achievements begin to hold meaning as symbols of the joy I was feeling internally.

The beauty is that there are two sides to every coin. So if it was *you* that made poor decisions based on flawed thought processes, that's great news! Now, you're aware and you can choose differently! However, if nothing was your fault and the world was to blame for everything, and you were merely a victim of your circumstances, you'd be screwed! There would be no opportunity to fix anything, no possibility of you ever achieving happiness or fulfillment. So the fact that you just didn't know any better means that you hold in your hands the key to your own joy, peace, happiness, and fulfillment. The key is called awareness. What's better than that?

Simply choose the other way. If you're choosing from fear, choose from love. If you're closing off when you experience something you don't like, choose to open. We don't screw up our lives because we're trying to; we screw up our lives because we don't know any better. We've been taught the wrong rules. Learn the right rules and begin to win at this game. It's fun when you know how to play! This is why everyone is teaching consciousness, mindfulness, awareness, presence, and being in the Now. It's all the same thing and it's extremely important. When we are living consciously, we make better decisions. When we know why we're doing what we're doing, we give ourselves the ability to choose differently to get different results. I wrote this book to give you a guide to having a happier, more fulfilling, and joyful human experience while you're here. Knowing that you have the ability to achieve that is huge!

Much of that knowing is having a simplified, consistent way of interacting with life that works. This is what spirituality provides. A system that works every time in every situation no matter how large or how small, how complex or how simple. This way of thinking is based on the laws of the Universe, the eternal, the ways that never change and have always worked. If you see someone successful at *anything*, there is spiritual law behind it. If you see a system that works consistently, there is spiritual law behind it. When you're able to begin making decisions from the foundation of love and fear, you can choose which direction to go easily. When you begin to live from the inside out instead of from the outside in—you experience consistent joy. It has *always* worked, and it will work for you.

PART 6

SELF-LOVE IS NOT SELFISH

Chapter 36

Self-Love or Frustration

Again, there are two main ways of doing things: out of self-love and out of frustration. Unfortunately, we've been conditioned through a system of punishment to curb our behaviors. This plays out in how we deal with things. Our focus is so external that we wait until we're frustrated with what's happening on the outside and we just can't take it anymore. Once we're at the breaking point, we attack whoever or whatever we perceive as blocking our happiness.

This leads into the attack and defend mode of communicating that most of the world practices. One side is pointing the finger and blaming, and the other side is defending. The actual problem is never truly looked at or considered. The main point is blame. Should there be blame? Who's to blame? They think it's my fault, but I don't think it's my fault. They did it, so it's their fault, they are to blame, etc.

The actual issue isn't the main topic; therefore, it is rarely addressed.

A healthy way to deal with behavior you don't enjoy is making it a matter of self-love. When things come from self-love, there isn't all the negativity or blame. We each have the right to determine our own experiences (for the most part). If someone is treating us in a way we don't like, we can make it about us and self-love. Instead of heading in with "You shouldn't talk to me like that," try "I can process information better without yelling. I find it more effective and enjoyable to work through things calmly and positively."

Self-love doesn't blame the other person; it states what you want. It's not about them. It's about you.

People have the right to yell, swear, get upset, and throw things. However, you have the right to not be treated like that. So instead of trying to change others—which usually ends up in blame and rebellion—simply state how you like to be treated. If someone yells at you, let them know that you don't do well when people yell at you. You choose not to engage or interact in that manner and walk away. Get yourself out of the situation. I've done this with relationships, with friends, with bosses, co-workers, etc. It's much more effective to act from a place of self-love rather than frustration.

It's a matter of energy, just like everything else. If you're in a situation with negative energy (which is usually why you're feeling uncomfortable), bringing in more negative energy in the form of frustration simply expands the problem. If you bring in love, it minimizes the problem.

It's easy to argue with someone who is frustrated. They are angry, not thinking clearly, and they're defensive; focused on a problem outside of themselves being thrust upon them by someone they can't control.

It's difficult to argue with someone who is focused on self-love. They are calm, in control, thinking clearly, and focused on what they can control (themselves).

The other person doesn't have to agree with what you're saying. That's not what you're asking of them. You're requesting that they don't treat *you* in a disrespectful manner because *you* don't like it. That's all. It's about *you* and what you prefer. How can someone argue with that? Are they going to disagree and say, "No, you actually *do* prefer what you just said you don't prefer"? That doesn't make sense. Of course, if someone is completely disrespectful and disconnected, they may take that approach. But, there's no sense in arguing with someone in that space, so it becomes clear very quickly that they're incapable of having a reasonable conversation. If someone is incapable of respecting your wishes or having a reasonable conversation on a regular basis, you may need to explore ways of not being around that person anymore. People like that are simply closed off and will probably continue to cause suffering to those around them. It's better to not be around them.

There are not as many people like that as you may think. Most people respond well to boundaries when they are put up in a loving, reasonable way. We must teach people how to treat us because they simply don't know. From our perspective, we can spend a lot of time thinking they should know because it's just common sense. In reality, most often people are moving so fast, they don't slow down enough to see how they're treating others from the other's perspective. They are focused on accomplishing what they want from their perspective. It's usually not true when they say, "I would never treat someone that way." The reason everyone feels that way is based on perspective. If you were too absorbed in your own reality and felt rushed and overwhelmed, you would probably treat someone in a way that's less than perfect. We've all done it. We usually disregard that because we rationalize it as necessary or "you would've done it, too" or "that was an extreme situation," or "they started it," etc. Often, we're so caught up in our own perspectives, we don't even know we've done it. So, how can we hold ourselves accountable for something we don't even remember doing? But boy, we're good at judging someone else when they don't treat us well.

I'm not saying that we allow it. But we do have to get off the high horse of thinking that we're better than them and that we've never done anything like that, because chances are, we have. Even if you haven't, it's not about the other person. They have the right to treat everyone in their lives like crap if they choose. And you have the right to not allow it. No one can feel happy treating others poorly, the punishment is built right in, manifesting in the form of unhappiness and eventually loneliness.

In extreme cases, people often say, "You don't understand. This person treats everyone that way." And I say, "No, they don't!" There is at least one person, perhaps it's a boss, a spouse, a child, a parent, or a friend, who they don't treat like that. Do you want to know why? Because that person won't allow it. Get on that list. Be on the list of people who simply won't allow it out of self-love. People only do what works. If someone can't hold a conversation with you or interact with you in a rude way because you won't allow it by ending the conversation, then eventually they'll stop. And yes, this is applicable in work situations, with ex-spouses, or even family members who have spoken to you that way for years.

When someone behaving rudely is addressed out of self-love, they can't defend their behavior. It's a difficult leap for them to say, "They *have* to let me yell at them and treat them disrespectfully." That's a difficult conclusion for someone to come to when they're seeing someone act out of self-love and not frustration.

Chapter 37

Setting Boundaries

Setting healthy boundaries is huge. We need to set boundaries with those around us, and then reinforce those boundaries as necessary. There are two key points to setting boundaries. The first one is understanding the person you're setting the boundary with does not have to agree with you. It's not about them; it's about you.

Everyone has two options: They can either decide to respect the way you wish to be treated, or decide not to interact with you. They don't have to agree with the way you'd like to be treated; however they do need to respect it. Don't make the discussion about whether the person agrees with your perspective or not; it's not about that. It's about them having enough respect for you to respect your wishes.

The second key point is that everything spiritual has to be a win-win for you. You know something is spiritual when it's a win-win situation. The win-win here is that they either treat you the way you want to be treated, or the interactions end (if possible) or are minimized depending on the situation. Every time you're treated in a way that goes against that, you walk away and don't even finish the interaction. Eventually, people stop doing what doesn't work and begin shifting the way the interactions go.

Be aware that boundaries are *a* spiritual act, but not the *only* spiritual act. They can be very empowering, but they also can be addictive. Once someone feels the power of how much control they have over their lives, they can get addicted to that power and misuse it. Remember, respect is a two-way street. So just because you can set boundaries, doesn't give you the right to disrespect others. The goal is to get along with others in a healthy way. It's not to run around setting boundaries with every Tom, Dick, and Harry that you feel like setting them with because the wind blew a certain way.

To have a healthy relationship with others, it requires communication, a sharing of ideas, and respect going both ways. So, respect the other person by taking the time to communicate your perspectives in the hopes that you can understand each other. Stay open to the possibility of a compromise. No one enjoys being in a relationship with someone who acts like it's their way or the highway and "I don't owe you an explanation. If you don't like it, tough." That's not loving, that's leaning too far in the other direction and becoming exactly what you're standing up against.

Exchange perspectives and learn from each other. At the end of it all, if there is no common ground, you have the right to set that boundary and hold it. It's your life, and ultimately your choice.

People don't have to agree with you and you can set your boundary anyway. It's simply a matter of respecting you, not agreeing with your perspective. The win-win is that people will either treat you in a way you'd like to be treated, or they won't be around mistreating you anymore.

Let's go deeper into why I say, "Everything spiritual is a win-win." To understand this, we can look at the fact that the Universe is always expanding, which means it's increasing in energy and size. The only way the Universe can expand is by its parts (the things that make up the Universe) expanding. Therefore, our growth helps it expand simply because we're part of it.

This expansion isn't random or a crap shoot. It happens consistently because that's the way the system is set up. The Universe is not set up in a way that one person has to give away 10 percent of their energy to help another person. That would mean there is a loss of 10 percent energy and a gain of 10 percent energy at the same time, so nothing would ever expand. Therefore, when you help someone unconditionally, it increases your energy. If that person accepts your help with love and uses it to better themselves, their energy also increases. This is a win-win!

We can see this play out in people who take joy in doing simple things for people. If they openly receive love while they're giving, they never burn out. It's a perfect system.

We don't have to be martyrs, giving until it hurts, and sacrificing all for others. That is a mentality of lack; like there's only so much good and if I give good to others, I must have less goodness in my life. The Universe is abundant with a never-ending supply of love and goodness. It never diminishes; it only expands.

Love yourself, be kind to yourself, and give from the overflow. Putting yourself last does not mean you're a good person; it means you're irresponsible. Many times, people keep giving to those who will take, and then wonder why the takers don't feel bad that you're doing without. They are mirroring what you're doing. If you are not taking care of yourself, you're being irresponsible, even when you're trying to help others. You're modeling how to be irresponsible and they are following your example. You're also enabling people to be irresponsible by not letting them experience negative consequences for their negative actions. Treating yourself responsibly and allowing others to be responsible too is a win-win for you both.

People need to feel the consequences of their actions, or else how are they supposed to find out what works and what doesn't work? Every time something goes wrong, we run around protecting people from the consequences of their actions, and then wonder why they keep repeating the same pattern. Stop helping people be irresponsible! That isn't love, it isn't kindness...it's enabling.

If you really want to show love to someone, show them what responsibility looks like, explain what they need to do if they're seeking advice, and then leave it up to them. Let them fall and get scraped up by life. Protecting people from feeling discomfort prevents them from learning. Discomfort, pain, and suffering are our guidance system, our bumpers. We're supposed to feel uncomfortable when doing the wrong things, that's how we know they're wrong. When we notice a feeling we don't like, we make an adjustment to not feel that again. Life is not supposed to be free of discomfort; it is the way we know what to do, how to grow.

Give people the information they need and lay out some actions for them to take. If they refuse to take the actions, allow them to experience the consequences of their choices.

I'm a parent, so I understand this is especially hard with your children, along with everyone else we care about: parents, relatives, and friends. With children, we must figure out our goal as parents. Look deeply into this. If you look closely, you'll notice the things most people follow literally don't make sense. Many parents complain that their children grow up too fast. And it's turned into what people perceive as an example of love. Often saying things like, "I wish they'd stop growing. They grow up too fast. Oh, this is horrible, I wish they'd stay little forever." Really? Is that what you want for your children? Is that what you want for yourself?

We do the same thing by sheltering our children from experiencing anything negative. "Someone called you a name? Well, you're not hanging out with them anymore. We'll go get them in trouble." We cannot expect to live in a world where no one ever treats our children badly. People will be mean, controversial, and unfair. Your children will be heartbroken when relationships break up. They will experience sadness, anger, and frustration, just as we all do. What will they do when this happens? That's what we need to keep in mind. We can't prevent our kids from experiencing anything negative, but we can teach them how to handle it when it does.

Don't try to raise a child who stays dependent on you forever and doesn't know how to handle adversity. Raise a child who can handle adversity—because there's plenty of it out there. Raise a child who doesn't need you because you won't always be around, and they'll need to rely on themselves. Look closely and make conscious choices about what you're teaching your children..

I know it's cute when your friends fawn over a picture of your child hugging a kitten and say, "I wish they could stay like this forever." If this wish were granted, you'll be paying their rent when they're 42 years old or raising their kids because they're incapable of doing it themselves. There are more ways than one to "not grow up." They'll grow physically because that's simply nature, but they will be mentally and emotionally stunted. So, we need to be conscious of how our lessons are training them for the future. If you look closely, it's not hard to see how this plays out. There are more adult children living with their parents now than ever before. And there are more grandparents raising their grandchildren than ever. This is not an accident. This is because parents are sheltering their children from learning how to be responsible for their own lives.

We must gain clarity of exactly what we're trying to do as parents. The main job of a parent is to raise an adult that is happy, joyful, independent, filled with self-love, and kind. Is that where your actions and attitudes are leading them?

Chapter 38

You Determine Who You Are

Don't let anyone determine who you are. Stand in your principles no matter what. Let's be clear…if you tell lies, then you are a liar. That is true, even if you feel you have a good reason.

Often, we rationalize our behaviors because someone did it to us first, or they deserve it, or the end justifies the means. It's all lies. The end doesn't justify the means. All you are is a sum of your "means." If you lie, you're a liar. If you cheat, you're a cheater. If you steal, you're a thief. Period. The circumstances don't change the facts.

So, if someone is attacking you, then walk away and set up a healthy boundary. If someone lies, tell the truth. If you need something, work for it or ask for help. Don't give other people or circumstances the ability to determine who you are as a person.

I understand this can be hard at times. I've been in situations where it looked like my son's welfare would be in danger if I told the truth and that he would benefit from a lie. At the same time, the other side was lying to prove their side of the situation. I had a decision to make: Do I put my faith in a man-made system and in the person on the other "side" of the situation? Or, do I put my faith in something that is more powerful than any of us and any system or situation I was in? I chose to live by spiritual principles and I told the truth. It wasn't always easy, but truth prevailed in the end, as it always does. Notice what I said: Truth didn't prevail in *every* little situation that I thought was important. But truth prevailed *in the end*, along with the fact that I love myself and who I am because of how I handled it.

I am one who is honest. I don't bend to pressures of negativity. I live by faith and not by sight. These things are more important than some of the little situations that seemed so important when I was going through them. There are no shortcuts to this work. There are no exceptions to self-love or faith. There are no good reasons to be bad. Choose to be good, stick to your values, and know that your external life will reflect your internal life if you stand true to who you are.

Chapter 39

Start Where You Are

We have all been alive for a while now—well, at least, long enough to have learned how to read or listen to this. During that time, we've had many experiences that led us to where we are. So, your past has determined where you are at this time. You have learned many things and implemented many of them into your life to arrive at this point. If you like where you are, you should continue using the things you've learned to keep you going in the direction you're going. If you do not like where you are, it's time to learn some new things and implement them in different ways than your past.

If you are experiencing an unfulfilling life, it's only because you haven't learned how to have a fulfilling one yet. We can *all* have a fulfilling life; it's just a matter of changing what's not working. I often refer to this quote by Albert Einstein: "You can't solve a problem with the consciousness that created it."

Many years ago, I faced the fact that my life was messed up, even though I had tried my best to find success and happiness. This meant that my best thinking didn't work, and I needed to learn a new way of doing things. Once I started learning a new way of thinking, it was like living in bizarro-world! Common sense became uncommon sense. The way I previously viewed things and solved problems was flawed. No wonder, it didn't work!

After learning a new way of looking at things through a series of perspective changes, life began to get a lot better. I found that I wasn't cursed or stupid or crazy; I was just lost without a map. When I learned that I was responsible for my past because of my poor decision making, I realized I could do better. I could create the life I wanted. It was the most empowering feeling I've ever had!

Don't allow your past to determine your future. You can begin where you are. You can learn a new way of Being that's fulfilling. Find someone who has what you want and ask them how they got it. Reach out to someone like a life coach to guide you, read more self-help or spiritual-based books like this, and listen to healthy podcasts that offer new ways of looking at things. Mine are called *Life, Lessons, & Laughter with Glenn Ambrose.* There are also many other ways to find free information about healthy ways of viewing things. The answers are out there, so begin your search for new information and your new life. You deserve it!

Chapter 40

Care for Yourself So You Can Better Care for Others

Many people have difficulty taking care of themselves and making themselves a priority. I saw it regularly as a personal trainer in my clients' physical lives and even more as a life coach in their spiritual lives. How do *you* take care of yourself? Do you allot time out of your day to stop and connect with a Higher Power? Do you take any time each week to give your body the exercise it needs? Are you a good example to your loved ones of caring for yourself emotionally? Mentally? Spiritually?

In your hectic life, it's easy to get carried away with "doing," and never find the time to just "Be." Most people usually are not still long enough to notice they're exhausted. Do you take steps to replenish your energy before it runs out? Your body, mind, and spirit will slow you down in one way or another unless you take care of them. You will suffer from sickness, stress, unhappiness, fatigue, irritability, and a variety of dependency issues. The sad part is that most people think living under these conditions is normal. We are *not* here to suffer—we are here to live!

When you care for yourself, you feel better physically, you're happier, you're capable of doing more, and you can care for others more effectively. One of the most important things you can do for the loved ones in your life is to be a living example of self-care. If you want your children to love themselves and take care of themselves, you need to show them how by doing it for yourself. This isn't easy, especially for parents who want to put their kids first. But all that is teaching them is to put others ahead of themselves. Of course, we must put them first in many situations; however, they also need to see us taking care of ourselves. Otherwise, how will they learn to do it for themselves?

To have peace in your life, see how you can best set your priorities as follows:

> **Source:** Put your Source of power first. Your Higher Power, the focus of your faith, the Divine Being that you believe in and depend on for meaning, peace, and love in your life, needs to come first.

> **Yourself:** Take care of you! If you don't take care of yourself, you'll be incapable of being the optimum expression of The Divine that you can be. Give yourself what you need to be happy, healthy, and connected.

> **Others:** Now that you've done the first two, you're capable of giving your best. Now you can be the best father, mother, child, brother, sister, friend, employer, or employee that you can be. You can excel at helping others and be an example of self-love, self-care, and a happy life!

I love the adage used in case of emergency before a plane flight. When the oxygen masks drop, put yours on *first,* and *then* put your child's on. If you're unconscious, you're of no use to anyone!

There's an unhealthy identity that good, loving people have a tendency to identify with—being a martyr. This is something we have to be cautious of as big-hearted people. It's easy to throw our self-care aside in the name of helping others and play the martyr. It's no wonder we get lost in this since we have very few examples of healthy living in society. Giving until your fingers bleed only leads to bleeding fingers.

If we are functioning at a 50 percent energy level, we only have 50 percent of ourselves to offer others. When we offer 50 percent of ourselves to others without caring for ourselves, that percentage drops lower. Eventually the body shuts down or the stress becomes so much that you have nothing to offer.

This doesn't make you a good person. This makes you a depleted person. However, if you care for yourself and give from the overflow, consistently refueling, receiving, and replenishing, you can give forever. The people that give the most are the ones that care for themselves first, thereby creating a never-ending supply of good to give.

This is why the idea of philanthropy that supports sustainable solutions is so wonderful. If we only throw money at a problem to alleviate suffering (which is sometimes necessary) without looking into a long-term solution to alleviate the problem altogether, we're missing the point. A problem is solved when a new way of doing things is put in place, not when the momentary suffering is paused. We must change the way things are done if we expect to transcend the issue. This is spiritual law and that's why it works in our personal lives, relationships, child-raising, schools, jobs and global issues. If it's spiritual, it works on *all* levels, in *every* situation.

Chapter 41

Spiritual Disciplines

For consistent growth, it's important to establish some structure and implement our spiritual disciplines. This statement can raise all kinds of fear and rebelliousness. I can rebel against myself if I'm not careful, so I know of what I speak! First I'm going to calm these fears, and then I'll address the statement.

We rebel against structure and discipline in our lives because of what they subconsciously represent. When I felt rebellious while attempting to implement some structure in my life, I decided to take a close look at it. I realized I was rebelling because I love the idea of freedom, and structure makes me feel like I'm restricting my freedom. Hmm, interesting I thought. So I took it further. Is this true? Does it restrict my freedom? In a way it does, but it doesn't seem like I'm feeling very free without the structure either, so what's the problem? Then, I looked at my life with and without structure to bring in some contrast for clarity's sake. First, I needed to be clear on what the life I wanted looked like. Here's my thought process:

> **The life I want:** I have the freedom of time and money to do the things that bring me joy: building the career I love, spending quality time with my son, having a social life, a romantic partner, and experiencing all the wonderful things the world has to offer while helping as many people as I can along the way.

> **Life without structure:** I'd already been living without structure and had little time or money to do

the fundamental things I wanted to do. I didn't have much freedom, even though subconsciously I thought I was making decisions based on a freedom mindset.

Life with structure: If I had structure, I could accomplish more which could free up time for enjoyment. I'd also be more productive, generate more income and be able to help more people. This is what I was denying myself in the name of freedom.

After doing my little dissection, I found that if I brought in some structure, it would result in the freedom I desired. Without any structure, I had no direction. Although I might feel free initially, it didn't result in my big-picture goals. I'll gladly bring in a little structure and relinquish the pseudo-freedom if it helps me achieve real freedom. To my surprise, I enjoyed the new structure. It helped me feel more focused and in control of my own life. Before, I felt like I was randomly doing things all the time and not accomplishing much. Now, I felt super productive *and* had more downtime. I was sold! Of course, I still design my life to have a fair amount of daily freedom. I can't completely abandon my sense of rebellion, but I've found that a fair amount of structure also serves me well. It's all about balance.

So, back to the spiritual disciplines. If you can get past "rebellion in the name of freedom," the largest block to structure, you can bring in some of the disciplines that will expand your growth and spiritual connection. The reason we have spiritual disciplines is because, like everything else, we're dealing with energy. If you want something to expand, you must feed it. If you want something to die off, you must starve it. If you'd like to expand your spiritual connection and all the happiness, joy, and fulfillment that comes with it, you must feed it regularly.

Spiritual disciplines include (but are not limited to) prayer, meditation, reading spiritual texts, listening to spiritual audios, watching spiritual videos, going to spiritual events with like-minded people, and engaging in spiritual discussions. Some people expand their spiritual lives through hobbies, art of any kind, being present with children or animals, being in nature, helping others, or through their work when it's done in a spiritual manner. People also expand their spiritual connection through acts of self-love like getting a massage, exercising, bringing home flowers, or simply being still.

It's not important what your spiritual disciplines are, as long as they work for you. I recommend at least some sort of prayer and meditation along with taking in new spiritual information daily from an external source such as a book, audio, or video.

You don't have to dedicate every waking moment to your spiritual walk. Remember the game is rigged in your favor. The Universe or a Loving God doesn't expect you to quit your job, ignore your needs, or those of your family to be happy. That would be denial of the human experience, which isn't helpful. There is no time in the spiritual realm, so you don't have to dedicate long periods of time to see results. It's more important to do short periods of time more often. This way, you can break out of the conditioned mind more regularly. The less time you spend wrapped up and lost in "doing", the better you'll get at "Being." Small, incremental breaks are extremely helpful. Sometimes I'll wear a bracelet and every time I feel it on my wrist (since I'm not used to it being there), I'll take a few seconds to center myself and feel the sensation of connection in my heart. Even if it's only two or three seconds, it counts. I've used many different games to remind myself of this. I've cut out little memes about gratitude from the Internet and taped them all over my house and car, stopping to feel gratitude for a moment each time I saw one. I've said a specific prayer twice while washing my hands or brushing my teeth. When I was constantly thinking about someone I missed, I began to connect to Divine Love each time they popped into my head, thereby replacing a feeling of emptiness with a feeling of love and fullness. There are many little tricks you can do to help you connect to your Source throughout the day.

As far as meditating, you can start with 5 or 10 minutes and build your way up to 20 minutes. At some point, you could do it twice a day perhaps. We all can do something. There's a saying: If you don't have time to meditate for 10 minutes, then meditate for 20 minutes—you simply must make time for your own peace. There are no shortcuts. If you expect to walk through this life with any level of consistent peace and happiness, you need to put energy towards it consistently. As you do, you'll find that it's not work; it's enjoyable and fulfilling. I love my spiritual connection time. It's the most wonderful part of the day. Sometimes, my brain tells me I don't have time for it or that it's a pain in the ass, but that's simply my ego attempting to regain control over my thinking. I understand that, so I don't take it seriously. I know the Truth. I know that connecting to my Source allows me to feel love vibrate through my entire being. Regardless of what circumstances may look like externally, I can connect and feel a level of safety, comfort, contentment, and peace that I can only find in the arms of my Divine Source.

Chapter 42

All Work Is Self-Work

This is something that comes up frequently. Basically, we are responsible for our own happiness. If you give that responsibility to other people or outside circumstances, things get rough. I don't believe in a Loving Creator that would create a world where our happiness is outside of our hands. If we have no control over our own happiness, that would mean our Creator doesn't love us and set us up for failure and misery. It just doesn't make sense.

So, if our happiness isn't based on our circumstances, it must come from within. I like using extreme examples to make a point because it's usually clearer to see, and then we can apply it to less extreme situations more easily.

Let's look at a romantic relationship. Often, people in a relationship blame the other for their unhappiness. If only they would do this or that...well, you know the drill. The fact is the only person we can change is ourselves. If we do the self-work necessary to find happiness, it won't matter if they do this or that. People think they need to fix the relationship, but the relationship is just made up of two people. The relationship isn't a "thing" that needs fixing; it's the people that make it up. The beauty of doing the self-work is that there are only two possible outcomes: the relationship continues or the relationship ends.

If you are doing the work on yourself and the relationship continues, it probably means that the other person did some of their own self-work, or you were more of the problem and you didn't see it. Another option is that you've found so much happiness from within that the things that were bothering you before don't even matter anymore. No matter what, you're happy and the relationship continues.

What if the relationship ends? Well, since you've done the self-work, you are a stronger, happier, and more capable person than ever before. The relationship ends and comes to its natural conclusion with less drama or fear. You can be thankful for the lessons you learned during this time and move on to happier, more fulfilling relationships. It's a win-win either way—must be spiritual!

This way of thinking applies to all situations. By doing the work on yourself, you will either shift the situation or have the strength and clarity to transcend it. Self-work improves our jobs, friendships, family situations, financial situations, and all the other situations that your ego says you can't possibly affect because they are external. It's amazing how much your ego can use your senses to fool you. "But this is about money," it says, or "But this is about someone I love," or, "But this has serious consequences," etc. This is spiritual law so it works every time, all the time. When you change, the situation changes too.

Once you focus on your inner self and connect to your Source, to Divine Wisdom, things begin to shift for the better. It has to, it's spiritual law. Sometimes the right idea comes to handle the situation, sometimes unexpected resources pop up or people suddenly become reasonable, and sometimes the problem somehow solves itself…it's mind-blowing!

The key is *really* surrendering, *really* going within, and *really* handing it over. If we simply pretend to hand it over in order to manipulate the Universe into fixing our problem for us the energy is completely different and it doesn't work. You can't fake energy, it's either True or untrue and vibrationally those are *extremely* different.

Chapter 43

Stop Playing the Victim

One of the most common ailments in our society is the victim mentality. This can play out in countless ways, with people thinking they have bad luck, they were born on the wrong side of the tracks, they're not getting the breaks, they can't get ahead, and so on. Quite honestly, we all do it to some degree. So, although you may know someone who does it constantly, don't be so quick to look at them and judge. Instead, look at your own life and see where it applies to you in your world.

We get so caught up in the problem, we forget that we have a choice about what we do in our lives. We have much more control over our lives than we realize. You don't have to stay at a job you don't like. You can start job searching for 30 minutes a day so you can find something else. You don't have to stay in an unhappy relationship. You can leave, even if it's complicated and takes a few months to figure out the logistics. Somewhere in the world, someone has been in the same situation as us with identical or worse circumstances and they get out of it. Take yourself out of the equation and pretend it's a friend coming to you for advice—what would you tell them? Get out of the problem and begin looking for the solution with an open mind. In most cases there is an abundance of options.

The problem is in the mentality. When feeling like a victim, we're so focused on the problem, we don't look for the solution. We feel sorry for ourselves, helpless, and trapped. As we focus on the unpleasant circumstances and feelings we constrict, tighten, and reinforce the so-called reality of the problem. As we stay focused on it, the problem gets bigger, we attach to things that reinforce it.

Often times a solution presents itself but we simply dismiss it as impossible because it doesn't line up with our negative thought process. We tell ourselves we're looking for a solution but we're so trapped in the problem, we come up with frivolous reasons why it won't work. When focused on the problem, your brain looks for things that support the problem. When focused on the solution, your brain looks for things that support the solution.

So, stop focusing on the problem and start looking for the solution. No one ever solved a problem by focusing on it. No excuses, no poor me, just facts. This is where I am...fact. This is called acceptance. Accept the reality of your situation without feeling sorry for yourself. "I'm here, in this situation. Of course I don't like it and I'll find a way to change it, but the fact is I am here right now. It's not permanent. It's temporary and changing just like everything else in this world. It's not good or bad, it simply is." Let all the self-pity fall away and look at it as a simple fact. "I don't like to eat peas and I also don't like the situation I'm in"—simple facts. Once you let go of the self-pity, you can begin to look for the solution and start gathering information. Look for possible alternatives and ask others for their perspectives or help. It comes back to Einstein's quote: "You can't fix a problem with the consciousness that created it." Oftentimes we need an outside perspective to help us see things in new ways. If you happen to be alone and cut off from others, you still have hope. You are connected to Divine Wisdom. Unique, creative, helpful thoughts can come to you whenever necessary. Often asking for help and other perspectives is simply easier. It's important to know that you're *never* stuck; there's always a way out. There has to be, in an ever-changing reality overseen by a Loving Creator, it's the only thing that makes sense.

There's a trick your ego does to stay in control and keep you stuck. It tells you to have all the steps figured out and see whether it's going to work before it's worth taking the first step. This is a lie, you don't have to have it all figured out. In fact, you most likely won't. If you do have a multi-step plan, unforeseen adjustments will need to be made along the way.

Determine the first step toward what you want and do that, then look for the next step and do that, etc. No one can see the future. You don't know what doors may open down the road, or even who you will become after taking the first couple of steps. We literally change as a person as we take each step. We become more hopeful, enthusiastic, and capable as we take each step. Therefore, the person taking Step 7 is not the same person standing in front of Step 1. Your brain is working differently. You're solving problems, you're seeing new opportunities, you're empowered, and it's exciting. Your self-love and self-confidence are growing, and you can accomplish more than you ever imagined!

So, stop looking at the problem and look for Step 1 of the solution. You haven't walked this path yet, so you won't be able to see how it's going to play out. Just know that you aren't meant to be unhappy and unfulfilled. Whatever you focus on expands. If you focus on the problem, it expands. If you focus on the solution, it expands—so focus on the solution. As you start walking in the direction of your dreams, you'll have the whole Universe conspiring in your favor to make it happen. Try taking the first step, you have nothing to lose but your unhappiness.

Chapter 44

Give People the Space to Dislike You

One of the most freeing things you can do is to give people the space to dislike you. It's amazing how much energy we spend attempting to get people to like us. We often pretend to have learned this lesson by saying things like, "I don't care what they think" or "If they don't like it, to heck with them." These statements are based in frustration, resentment, and build a wall against someone that's hurt our feelings. The day we can say "Yes, I understand they view me as a bad person, and I'm fine with that" completely out of love and not frustration, that's when we become free.

There are many different people in this world and different perspectives for each person, built on things we'll never fully understand. Basically, what happens is our experiences mesh with our personalities and are processed in specific ways based on who we are and what we experience.

Here's an example. If you take a crayon away from two different children, you can get two different responses: One child gets upset and cries because you took their crayon, and the other child just grabs a different crayon and starts using that one, assuming you needed the first one.

It's the same experience with two different reactions, based on their individual personalities and how they process things. Now, picture it happening billions or trillions of times over the course of a lifetime. Each experience is processed in someone's unique way with multiple experiences varying dramatically with each person. This infinitely complex process is what creates each person's perspective, the lens through which they view the world. It's mind boggling to comprehend, and there's no way we could ever fully understand the intricacies of someone's perspectives and where they originated. The person themselves doesn't even understand where their perspective comes from. So, if they aren't even aware of why they think a certain way, how can we possibly have the information necessary to judge them for it? We can't. That's called being prejudice. Pre-judging. Judging without all the information. We can never fully understand why someone thinks or arrives at certain conclusions, so deciding on whether they "should" or "should not" be seeing things a certain way is a moot point. We don't have their perspective, so who are we to judge? And if we judge everyone who sees things differently than us as wrong— we're in even bigger trouble. There's no chance to find peace with that mentality.

Another thing we must consider is the way people interact with the reality around them. We unconsciously select the information we choose to absorb from each situation. It's been said that we are exposed to approximately 11 million bits of information per second and the human brain can only process around 40 of them. That leaves a lot of room for interpretation. One person will see the color of the wall while another will notice the picture, the clock, or the crown molding in the top corner. There are endless possibilities! So, if we take that variation and combine it with the trillions of experiences that are meshed with our personalities and how we process those experiences, there are countless ways to view the exact same situation.

When you take all these components into consideration, along with how people interact with the reality around them, you can begin to understand the big picture. Many disagreements happen because each person feels they have the right to judge and determine what is right, wrong, and how other people are supposed to view things. We need to allow people to have their perspectives, improve our own communication, and not assume we know why someone has a different perspective than us. Let them have their perspective. It's okay. We're not all supposed to have the same one.

In many situations (especially when emotion is involved), people will disregard information that doesn't support what they're looking to prove. It's true that whatever you look for, you will find.

If you look for a problem, you'll find one. If you look for a solution, you'll find one. If you want to believe someone is a bad person, even if you're shown a reason they're a good person, you'll simply dismiss that information. You'll say it's not important or not true—whatever you need to in order to continue believing what you want to believe. It happens all the time. If you ask people if they do that though, they'll likely say "no."

That's because it's an unconscious act. Most people aren't present enough to decide what they want for dinner, let alone know why they're making snap judgments on a regular basis. They are sweeping certain information aside while latching onto other information. This is why you can develop a "study" to prove anything you want. Just look for the information that supports and proves your point, while dismissing the rest. If you focus on a specific area, it will expand as the rest fades away. We need to keep and open mind and consider multiple perspectives without latching onto one as the truth, just because it matches what we believe.

A wonderful line that touches on this is: *A mind is like a parachute; it only works when it's open.*

The Dalai Lama stated that he has been accused of being non-committal in certain situations or flip-flopping on an issue. He explained that when someone is speaking to him, he listens and tries to see their point of view. As he sees it, he says "Yes," "I understand," "good point," etc. Then he will listen and respond in the same manner while someone else explains an opposing view. He's not waffling; he's actively listening and trying to understand what each person is saying. After hearing multiple sides, he retains the right to weigh them and come to his own conclusion. It doesn't mean the other people are wrong. It just means he decided one aspect was more appropriate to align with his personal way of thinking than other ways. Most often, his way of thinking is based in compassion and love, which is why he has connected with so many people around the world.

Understanding that there are many people, all with their own perspectives, and we're not all supposed to see things the same way is paramount to our happiness. We must make room for other people to perceive things differently. It's okay if someone thinks you're a horrible person, there are people who think I'm horrible, they've told me. I experience a tremendous amount of peace by accepting that and understanding that just because they think it, doesn't mean I agree with it or that it's true. It's just their perspective based on their own past experiences meshed with experiences with me, and interwoven in a tapestry that neither of us can fully understand. And we don't have to understand it, it is what it is. Needless to say, I don't spend time with these people or interact with them—why would I? There's about 8 billion people on the planet, I'm not supposed to get along famously with all of them. I give them the space to live their lives without judgement and I take the space to live mine. It's literally inconsequential to my world—this is freedom. When you come to a place where something that used to bother you is now a non-issue, you've found freedom from it. If you have to continue protecting yourself from it or fighting against it, it still controls you.

Lean into the spiritual terms like acceptance, allowing, and letting go. Allow people to have their beliefs even though you don't agree with them. As long as it's not affecting your life, who cares? If it is affecting your life, you may need to go back to the boundary-setting chapter or use a different tool to shift the situation. Regardless of what you need to do, you can live in a world where people disagree with and dislike you, without carrying the resentments and anger that tie you down and bind you in unhappiness.

Chapter 45

Handling Arguments

There are three main groups of people: people who see; people who see when they are shown; and people who don't see, even when they are shown.

People-who-see live mostly consciously. They usually have opened through some sort of suffering. They are grounded, they interact through love, and try very hard to be good people in almost every way. There are also more and more people being born with a tendency for openness, so it's becoming more common nowadays.

People-who-see-when-they-are-shown are close to opening on their own with a little guidance. They have specific traits in common with people-who-see, such as open-mindedness, honesty, and willing-ness. They are open to seeing things differently and not hung up on their current paradigm. They have the capacity to be honest with others; but more importantly, they have the capacity to be honest with themselves, even when it's uncomfortable and downright painful. They also are willing to change, see things differently, and implement their new perspectives in ways that enhance their lives.

Lastly, there are people-who-don't-see-even-when-they-are-shown. Most of these people will never open in this lifetime. Either they simply aren't supposed to, or they experienced things in their life that closed them so tightly that they're not capable of opening. Of course everyone has the ability to open if the conditions are right and they choose to; it's just very unlikely with this group. As more people open and the collective vibrational atmosphere becomes that of more love, it's possible they will feel safe enough to open.

Again, it's unlikely and trying to change them is an exercise in futility. You must meet people where they are with acceptance, and interact with them accordingly.

This mindset is important because most of the arguing that keeps society stuck takes place between the people-who-see and the people-who-don't-see-even-when-they-are-shown. They are on two different sides of an issue and they constantly attack each other. They try to get the other side to see things their way, usually by putting them down. That never works. When was the last time someone called you an idiot, told you that what you were doing was stupid, that you were stupid, and that everything you stand for is stupid; and then all of a sudden, you thought "You're right! Thank you so much for enlightening me, I never realized how stupid I was! Is there a group that I can join so I can spend more time with people like you?" That never happens! We get offended and stand our ground even more.

So, let go of the arguing. You're not going to change anyone on the other side. What you can do is keep working on yourself and put out information to support your way of thinking without attacking the other side. People who are open to change are looking for things that make them feel better. Arguing doesn't make them feel better. Things that make them feel better are love, acceptance, peace, and joy. Show those things and be an example of what you are trying to promote. When you meet someone that has interest, you can explain, provide information, and welcome them. You don't have to turn them into foot soldiers in your war on something. Love spreads, it feels good, and we all want it. It's better to attract, rather than provoke. Be the change you wish to see, and then watch all those people-who-see-when-they-are-shown come over to the side of love.

We cannot change the world by arguing with people who have no interest in changing. We must be an example of love and acceptance to those that are looking. All we need is 51 percent to reach the tipping point. When there are more people focused on love than on arguing, a dramatic shift will take place. And if you are one who wants love but is spreading hate by attacking others that don't agree with you...look at what you're really doing. Hate is hate. It doesn't matter if you feel justified in it, because it's the same energy.

You cannot *fight* for peace. We've been fighting for peace for thousands of years; it doesn't work.

I'm not saying dismantle all the armies tomorrow. I understand a world shift of this magnitude will take time, but we need to start walking in the direction of this change in our own lives and, eventually, the collective society will reflect that. Right now, we point our fingers at the government and complain about what they're doing, while we do the same thing on a smaller scale in our everyday lives. We talk behind people's backs, character assassinate, lie, cheat, steal, hurt, and argue. We focus on what we can get, instead of what will bring us peace. Then, we wonder why the government does the same thing. It's a reflection of us. If there were more people acting loving, our government would represent that and be more loving. And if it didn't, we'd simply vote them out. Things can change, but it starts with us first: in our homes, in our workplaces, and in our lives.

We must live consciously. We must slow down and look at the reasoning behind our actions, instead of taking them because they sound neat in a meme. Just because it's catchy, doesn't mean it makes sense. Most of the things we do in our lives literally don't make sense. This is why I love spirituality so much. When I look at what I used to do, it didn't hold water or make sense. "I love my son, so I'll protect him from as much as I can" sounds wonderful, but it doesn't actually make sense. If I loved him, I would want what's best for him. And what's best for him? To learn there are no consequences for his actions? To not learn how to handle disappointment? To learn that if he doesn't try, I'll do it for him? Of course not. What's best for him is to learn from his experiences, not to be sheltered from them. Look deeper into what you're doing and make sure it makes sense before you make it part of your life.

Part of living consciously and with purpose is knowing when and how to minimize arguments. I've been in social situations with people who obviously disagreed with my perspectives and wore their point of view like a badge of honor. The first words out of their mouths were to establish how opposite their stance was to mine. I would make a point of giving them the right to their perspectives without bothering to voice mine, thereby avoiding a useless argument. After these conversations, people have come up to me and said things like: "Why didn't you straighten them out?" Or,

"You could've proved them wrong so easily, why didn't you?" I tell them it's because they weren't interested in my point of view. They were locked onto their own views and it was very obvious they weren't open to change based on what they said and how they said it. Therefore, why should I waste my time debating something with someone who has no interest in what I have to say? I gave them the space to believe what they wanted because I wasn't going to change their mind anyway; it would have been an exercise in futility.

It can be exciting when you meet the people-who-are-open to-see-when-they-are-shown. This is when I'm happy to get into in-depth discussions about the intricacies of things. You can feel it when you're talking with someone that is absorbing your words—not necessarily agreeing with all of them, but open and absorbing them. There is an effortless and non-defensive exchange of ideas and thoughts. The conversation flows and gets more enjoyable as it goes regardless of whether you're both on the same page or not. It's an exchange of energy, not an exercise in who's right and who's wrong. You can walk away with tremendous respect for someone after an exchange like this, even knowing they don't agree with your perspectives. It's not about agreement, it's about a non-judgmental exchange of ideas while respecting each other's freedom to believe whatever you want to believe.

Most wars are not fought because people disagree with each other. They are fought because people disagree with each other and also refuse to allow each other to have their own perspectives. If we simply allowed people to live from their own point of view, many wars and arguments would be avoided. This is part of where I see us going in the future.

Chapter 46

Little Victories

The most common hurdles faced in life are unconscious expectations and viewpoints that simply don't make sense when brought to the light of consciousness. People unconsciously expect to live their lives with nothing but victories, with no setbacks, and always be able to handle vast amounts of external and internal pressures without feeling overwhelmed. If they feel overwhelmed or experience a setback, then something must be wrong with them, the situation, or both. This is just unrealistic. Many people don't realize they're doing this, but if we look deeply into what bothers us on a daily basis and why—we'll see the truth of it.

Life consists of a series of moments and experiences. You are in an experiential place interacting with an ever-changing reality. You're supposed to experience different things that push you to grow and move you toward a higher version of yourself. In life, you'll experience a myriad of things, and the joy is in the journey.

The journey has everything including setbacks, but you're not supposed to focus on them. You're supposed to focus on the little victories along the way and simply learn from the setbacks. The little victories are the fun of life. If you push those aside, what do you have? Where can you find motivation, joy, and purpose?

You will succeed more than you fail. If your focus is fixated on your little victories, you'll see that they add up to large victories, goals being reached, and joy experienced all along the way. That's how it's supposed to be, a joyous journey of excitement and experiences; knowing all the while that you are safe, your best is good enough, and that you are loved and supported beyond measure.

No one ever leapt to the top of a mountain. They took one step at a time, and each step was a small victory. If they focused on the times they slipped and went backwards, they'd never reach the top. There are small victories every day, even if it's just getting out of bed. If you did that, congratulate yourself. If you didn't, then attempt it tomorrow. If you're bedridden, start a blog or watch a video with a good message. Do something positive, and then congratulate yourself for it. You deserve the joy that comes along with it!

When you focus on the positive, you will experience more positives. This is why you gain energy and feel good when you focus on victories, and why you lose energy and feel negative when you focus on failure. It's the system. You will feel good and energized when you do something that's beneficial to yourself and others. You will feel bad and lethargic when you do something that's detrimental to yourself and others. This is your guidance system, so use it. Do what makes you feel better. You're worth it and deserve to experience the joy that is in the journey!

Chapter 47

Life Happens for Us, Not to Us

Let's start with a quote: *"Life moves pretty fast. If you don't stop and look around once in a while, you could miss it."*
~ Ferris Bueller's Day Off

Life does go by fast, and the first thing we need to do to turn negatives into positives is slow down so we can make some adjustments. Instead of rushing from one thing to another and absorbing the negativity of countless situations, we need to pay attention to how we're looking at things. Little things like getting stuck in traffic, dropping something, or even getting sick. Very often, these messages are trying to capture our attention, so we can make the necessary adjustments before something bigger happens. The messages are usually life lessons like: slow down; take care of yourself; don't take things so seriously; laugh more; check your priorities and live by them.

When you look at happy and successful people, you'll notice they usually don't see a negative thing as a problem; they see it as an opportunity to make a needed adjustment. They view it as information they can use to do things better. This is a highly effective way of thinking, as opposed to seeing every negative situation as a roadblock.

If we can slow down and learn to use the negative things as learning opportunities, we'll see that life happens *for* us, not *to* us. The next time something negative happens, you can stop and think: "I don't believe there's a Creator up there who loves me and is needlessly throwing negative situations at me. There must be something I can learn here." Then, find the lesson. How can this negative situation benefit me and my life?

We must remember that our perspective is limited. Often we are too quick to judge things with the minimal information we have available at the time. When I first opened to this mentality years ago, I began to experiment with it (as I like to do). I noticed there was a two-week window for me. Anything that went in a way that I perceived as "wrong" or "bad" at the time would turn into something "good" within two weeks. It was amazing! I just needed to give things a little space and see how they unfolded to understand the big picture. This is the perspective we need to keep in mind—it's the chaos theory. Everything looks chaotic until you step back far enough to gain perspective. If you were to stand an inch away from a world map, you'd be missing most of the world. Take a few steps back and you see there's a much bigger picture there.

There is a Loving Creator with a view that's much broader than ours, that has access to information we don't. Try to trust the Loving Creator with the bigger, better view! When I looked at the circumstances of my life before I got sober and woke up, they were tragic. I was homeless, addicted to alcohol, my body was shutting down, my son was 1400 miles away from me, I was unemployable, and I was broke. That sucked! Those were also the conditions which pushed me to the awakening that changed my life and helped me to become the happy, healthy person I am today. Without experiencing the level of discomfort and pain those circumstances brought me, I never would have been able to open to the love and joy I've experienced. I wouldn't be the father I am or capable of helping the people I help. I also wouldn't have written this book. They say hindsight is 20/20 and I couldn't agree more. Given a little, time, space, and perspective we begin to understand that things are always working for us, not against us.

With this thinking, you'll start being thankful for the lessons, instead of being a victim of the circumstances. Start with something small and train yourself to look for the positive. It's worth it for the sake of your own happiness!

Chapter 48

Act Yourself into Better Thinking

You can't think yourself into better acting; you must act yourself into better thinking. This is a lesson I learned many years ago, and I have found it to be true in many situations. So often, we'll sit at home thinking about what we need to do, or what it would be like if our situation were different, or decide to wait until it "feels right." We're waiting for the motivation to do something different. Often we're waiting because we can't mentally comprehend achieving the result we want from where we are. You can't see the last part of the journey until you get there. The fact is you get stronger as you move, as you take action. You gain knowledge as you experience more. You're not the same person with the same perspectives after taking action. There's a little more hop in your step, a little more confidence, energy, positivity and all these things make you a little more capable of doing something that you're not capable of doing from where you're sitting now. And sometimes what looked like an obstacle was merely fear and once we faced it (even though we swore it was real), it turned out to be nothing.

You see, the reason you aren't moving is because you are stuck. Don't sit around and think about what you should be doing but don't have the motivation to do. Just get up and start doing it! It's going to be difficult, it's going to take effort, and you'll probably feel like you don't want to do it. That's all because you're not in the rhythm of doing. When a car is stuck in the mud, it cannot move forward. It takes some effort to push it out of the rut and get it moving forward. But, as soon as it's out of the rut, it wants to take off. That's how you'll feel when you push your way out of being stuck!

Take action by starting with the first step, and then take the second one, and soon you'll be out of the mud and moving forward. Don't wait until it feels right, because it won't. An object at rest stays at rest—unless it kicks itself in the ass and gets moving! So, kick yourself in the butt and take some action, even if you don't feel like it. Become the object in motion that stays in motion! There's so much for you to do and experience in this world. Don't wait until the ride is over to realize you missed all the fun.

PART 7

BEING THE CHANGE

Chapter 49

The Moment of Change

What does it look like and feel like when your life shifts for the better? You know...those ah-ha moments, those epiphanies, those light bulb moments people talk about. They sound very elusive, but they are quite simple in structure. Basically, it's just a shift of perspective. The reason they can sometimes be so profound is when it's a shift of perspective at the core of an issue and suddenly you're looking at things from a different perspective, then everything attached to it changes.

For example, if you believe that you're incapable of learning new things, it can be very discouraging and detrimental. If you then find out that you have a learning disability and begin to consume information in a different way that works for you—it can change your life! You could begin to follow your passion because now you believe you can learn what's necessary to succeed. You could become very successful and more confident along the way. Perhaps confident enough to ask out the person you like and find out they feel the same way. You could end up raising a family together and experience much joy throughout your life. This all stemmed from a change of perspective. The facts of the situation did not change, only the perspective. Once your perspective shifted, you began to interact with life differently and it snowballed into a completely new way of Being. This happens more often than we realize.

Spiritual awakenings eluded me when I believed they were lightning bolts from God or an overwhelming God-consciousness. These things seemed so profound and large that I couldn't comprehend experiencing them. However, when I understood that it was just a matter of changing how I looked at things, they became possibilities...and then realities.

I looked back on my life and saw that perspectives can change. There were things that I thought were true, and ways of thinking I depended on previously that had changed over time. When these perspectives changed, the way I interacted with life changed along with them. This is what provided an opening for more and more perspective shifts to occur within me.

In recovery, I learned that there are three things needed for change, and these things are indispensable. They are open-mindedness, honesty, and willingness. This has worked for millions of alcoholics and addicts worldwide—the reason is because it makes us receptive to a shift of perception. We need to be open-minded to understand there might be another way to look at things. We need to be honest with ourselves to understand the way we're looking at things is not working for us and start taking responsibility for our own lives. And we need to be willing to try something different.

The "moment of change" does not have to be elusive, I see it daily with my clients. Most people don't seek out a life coach until they're ready to change and are in possession of the three traits needed for change: being open, honest, and willing. Offering up a different perspective to people who are open to it is basically what I do for a living. No wonder I love it so much!

Here's a small exercise you can do with this information or with anything you're trying to gain clarity on. Sit and become still, focus your attention on your heart area, perhaps putting your hands over your heart. Then ask yourself each question five times (or more if necessary), going deeper and deeper each time while listening for the answer in the stillness of your heart. First ask yourself: Am I open-minded? Am I really open-minded? Am I really, really open-minded? Pausing between each question to listen and adding a "really" in front of each one. Eventually the True answer will reveal itself and you'll feel the Truth of it inside yourself. It will be different from a mental answer and will be coming more from within your body than your head. This is a wonderful way to enhance the connection with yourself, your Source, and the deep Truths inside of you. This practice will increase the honesty you have with yourself, and help you find out what you need to focus on to become a fuller version of yourself.

Understanding that "moments of change" are simply changes of perspective make them much more attainable. Learning to go within to find the Truth inside you also enhances the process. It's important to know that these moments occasionally come as powerful realizations and more often, they come little by little in the form of learning something new and implementing it in your life. The most common is a combination of both, mostly learning a little at a time with an occasional big ah-ha moment. No matter how they happen, the important thing is that these "moments of change" happen and happen regularly. This is what changes your vibration to a happier, healthier, more conscious You. So when you experience them, embrace them, internalize them, and hold them dear—they come from within and therefore hold the key to your happiness.

Chapter 50

Being the Best Version of Yourself

Everyone wants to be the best version of themselves. It's natural. Our nature is to expand, grow, and become more of ourselves. But how? I'm going to let you in on a little concept that should help: You already are the best version of yourself, right now.

Let's look at this closely. What does "being the best version of you" mean? It means you are capable of living, acting, and functioning in a way better than you previously did. It doesn't mean you did everything perfectly today, or that you're a worse version of yourself because you did things well last year and things aren't going as well right now. Sometimes we have good days or stretches, and sometimes we have difficult days or stretches. This is not a reflection of our capabilities.

Being the best version of yourself means that you are capable of functioning at a higher level. So, if you've had one more bad day than you had previously, or one more broken relationship, one more breakdown and cry episode, or one more thought pass through your mind that you don't want to keep living like this, then congratulations! You are one step closer to shifting what you want to shift, experiencing that last straw that drives you to true surrender, and opening to a new level of peace. You are one step closer to finally making the decision that your happiness is worth more than maintaining the status quo and finally being ready to seek help.

And if you've had one more good day, congratulations! You are one step closer to finding what works for you, creating the road map to find your way back to happiness, and getting comfortable with the vibration of joy so that it becomes your new normal.

With just one more passing day, you are better because you have one more day of experience on which to base your decisions. When your ego says, "Here you are again, a year later, and you haven't grown at all," you can recognize that for what it is—a lie. Your ego is trying to keep you stuck! Just the sheer fact that you had one more year of trying makes you more capable of transcending whatever you're trying to transcend. Don't fall for the lie. You *are* improving and you *can* be who you want to Be. If you need to dig deep to make a change you haven't made yet, start digging. This time you're much more likely to find what it takes than the last time you went digging.

So, get excited for today. Being here today means you're that much more capable than you were yesterday of living the life of your dreams. At this moment, you are the best version of you that you have ever been in your entire life!

Chapter 51

Your Best Is Good Enough, It Has to Be

There is so much pressure to make the right decision and do the right thing that it's exhausting and quite frankly, not much fun! The Truth is that our best is always good enough. The Universe's system isn't based on how well you scored like society's system has taught you; it's based on earnest desire. When I was going through my wake-up process, I was a complete mess. I had abused my body and mind with negative thinking, victim mentality, extreme rationalization, drugs and alcohol, poor nutrition, etc. I was incapable of doing a "good job" at anything, especially straightening out my life!

However, I had profound spiritual awakenings that were brought on by a combination of my utter exhaustion and my unwillingness to live the way I was living any longer. I simply refused to continue with the way things were. With this motivation, I applied what I was learning with complete abandon. I didn't care or worry if it was going to work, how it was going to work, or even if it made sense. I simply did it to the best of my ability. And it worked amazingly well!

As others saw me change, they thought I was amazing and that I had done so much to change. Sure, I did my part to the best of my ability, but my ability level at that time was horrendous. My positive results were based on my willingness to change, and that's why the change took place. It wasn't based on my capabilities. And I wasn't the one that made the changes. For lack of a better explanation, I simply opened, allowed, and let go of thought processes that I'd been living by. I didn't make anything happen. I got out of my own way and allowed it to happen through me by a Loving force much greater than me.

Our progress is not determined by our capabilities. It's determined by our willingness to let go and allow the nature of our True selves to arise from within. We already have everything we need to succeed; the seed is contained within us. Everything a tree needs to become a mighty oak is contained within the seed. It is within you!

If you want to stay the course, it's also important to understand that your best varies from day to day. The ego attempts to keep us stuck by tricking us. It says that you're getting worse, you're making no progress, and shows us evidence of days we did better in the past. As we compare our bad day to a better day in the past, we say: "Oh no, I am getting worse!" The reason this doesn't make sense is because we constantly fluctuate between good days and bad days, between good stretches and bad stretches. Can you imagine if you went to work and had a perfect day where everything went right, then your boss judged every day thereafter based on that day? You'd never live up to it and probably be fired within the month. Yet this is what our ego attempts to do to us. We have to look closely to see what makes sense and what doesn't before we believe in it.

Now that you understand the ego's trick, you can focus on your commitment level. We must commit to change. The ego has been crafting its excuses for years within you, and society reflects the wrong way back to you from every direction. Commitment is what breaks through all of this. If you look closely, you'll find that leaning into the commitment is easier than you think. All you're protecting is your right to be unhappy—that's the only thing you're risking. When you begin to understand that you do deserve happiness and all you're risking is your unhappiness, you can fully lean in. Right before people awaken, the most common mindset is this: "I refuse to live like this any longer."

So make the commitment to lean in, to constantly move forward, even if it gets difficult. I can tell you from personal and collective experience—you are good enough. Your best is good enough. You are capable of achieving the happiness you so deserve. That nudge that got you to read this book is right, keep following it. Sometimes your best will be lying in bed crying all day. Sometimes it will be having a phenomenal day and helping people while experiencing the flow of joy, peace, and love all at the same time. Many times it will fall somewhere in between. But the commitment is to consistently do your best, whatever it is that day, and never stop moving forward. You're worth it.

Chapter 52

Walking Through Fear

Fear has a way of holding us back from accomplishing what we want in life. The silly part is that fear is just an illusion. It's not a "thing." Most of us have walked through some sort of fear in our lives and done something we were afraid to do. Later, if you looked back to see the fear that had been blocking you, you would see and feel nothing. The fear is not there.

It's not there because it's illusory. It's just a belief system that we agreed to at some point. If you're afraid of something, there is someone who is not afraid of it. That's not because they are better than you or more capable than you are. It's because they didn't buy into the way of thinking that believes they are afraid.

Fear is simply a mindset, and we can change what we believe. The answer is expanding your mind to believe that impossible things are possible. That is what Alice in Wonderland did when she was fighting the Jabberwocky. She recited the six impossible things that happened to her before breakfast. This expanded her mind to believe that she could slay the Jabberwocky, even though she was a little girl standing up to a huge monster.

Changing our mindset can be done, but it still takes courage to walk through the illusory fear. After you do it once, you have the physical proof that you're capable of pushing past fear, and now you're more likely to do it again. Start with something small with small consequences and walk through your fear. Then, work up to something larger.

The opposite is also true: If you allow fear to control a part of you, it will attempt to control more of you. So, next time you're thinking about letting fear win, understand that it's taking up residency inside you and will continue to take over more space if you allow it.

No one starts out completely fearful, it begins small, and then expands. As a child we can be fearful of the dark and then of spiders. If left unchecked we can eventually add things to the list like: fear of crowds and public places which can morph into life as a recluse. It happens. No one is born with all these fears, they gradually take over more and more of someone's life. Wherever you are, stop now and reverse the curse. Little by little, you can reclaim your life. You deserve to be in control of it, not in fear of it.

Mark Twain said: "Courage is resistance to fear, mastery of fear, not absence of fear."

Fear lives in the unexamined space. Fear says: "Glenn, you can't start a business as a single parent with no savings and not enough income to pay your bills! What if you fail? What if it doesn't work out?" As long as I stay in the "what if" space—fear has me. They are good points! To prevent fear from controlling you, you must follow the thoughts through to their conclusion. What would actually happen if I failed or it doesn't work out? Then I'll get a job somewhere. I've been unemployed before, many times in fact, and I've always ended up with a job. What if you end up sleeping in your car? Then I'll get lots of blankets and have my son stay at his friend's house for a few weeks until I can get a job and an apartment for us. It'll suck, but I'll make it. I've been in difficult situations before and I've always made it—I'll make it this time too (if it happens).

When fear comes up, I play "worse-case-scenario." Let's get it all on the table, what's the worst thing that can happen? If that happens, I'll deal with it. Once I stand in the worse-case-scenario and realize I can handle it, my fear doesn't have a leg to stand on. The important thing is realizing you can handle it. Notice I didn't say "like" it. I wouldn't have "liked" sleeping in my car and my son not having a home but we would've made it. You can't allow what you wouldn't "like" to freeze you. You don't "like" where you are now, otherwise you wouldn't be debating a move that brings up so much fear.

If you stay where you are now, you'll definitely be unhappy. You know this because you're unhappy now. If you try something different, you might end up in a situation you don't like or you might end up in one you do like, at least there's a chance. Where you are now, there's no chance.

The worst thing we can do is not move. It goes against nature and Universal law. Everything is expanding, changing, growing, evolving, and moving. Non-movement = depression. When we don't move, the flow of our life-force slows down, our energy gets depleted, and our confidence drops. It gets harder and harder to move. An object at rest tends to stay at rest. If you've been stationary and frozen by fear, it's time to see it for what it is—an illusion, and break free.

We all experience fear in many forms, there's nothing wrong with experiencing it. Letting fear control us is the problem. We must learn to stand in it and move forward anyway. Fear is nothing in and of itself, it can't hurt us. Only our reaction to fear can hurt us. Stand in your power, know that it is illusory and can't hurt you, become the master of your own fate.

Chapter 53

Silence: The Gateway to Source

Silence is around every noise, underneath every sound, and waiting at the end of every echo. Speaking from a mental construct, you can say that silence is "what isn't," as opposed to "what is." In life, our attention is drawn to what is and what stands out, but what is behind all the sounds that are standing out? Silence.

To better understand silence, we can compare it to space. The space in your living room is no different in this example than outer space. Space is nothing, not a "thing." Your couch, walls and floor are all things but the space between them is not a thing. This is the same as silence. It's what's between the sounds. Objects and things like sound capture our mental attention, but if we focus on space and silence, we can sense that Source is within them—the Source of everything that has ever been, is now, and ever will be. Everything that has form rises out of the seeming nothingness. The Source of everything is in the *no-thing-ness*. It's not a thing; it's what all things come from. So if we focus our attention on silence or space, we can experience what the Buddha refers to as Noble Silence.

Every religion and spiritual practice talks about silence being a gateway to Source. Here are just a few:

> Be still and know that I am God. ~ *Psalm 46:10*

> Now be silent. Let the One who creates words speak. He made the door. He made the lock. He also made the key. ~ *Rumi*

You can hear the footsteps of God when silence reigns in the mind. ~ *Sai Baba*

Since connecting to our Source is what allows us to experience the love, safety, and peace that we all seek, silence should be a cherished archway to bliss that we pass through often. There is nothing you need to learn, find, acquire, or gain. The silence is always there, always waiting for you to give it your attention and connect to all that you seek.

Chapter 54

Forgiveness

Here's a big one, folks. It's forgiveness. This is one of the most misunderstood concepts and it results in an immense amount of suffering!

The first thing we need to comprehend is that forgiveness is *not* about letting the other person off the hook. It does not mean there are no consequences. It does not mean you agree with what they did, or that you're saying it's okay that they did it.

Forgiveness is about letting *yourself* off the hook. It is about accepting the reality of what happened and not wasting time and energy wishing things happened differently. They didn't happen differently; they happened the way they happened. Wishing things could have been different is completely futile. It accomplishes nothing but suffering.

All you are saying to yourself when you forgive someone is that you accept the fact they did this in the past. You understand that it's impossible to go back in time and change it, and you're going to move on. You can still hold people accountable in different ways, depending on the circumstances. You can decide to no longer loan them money, no longer trust them with sensitive information, or no longer associate with them, etc. The point is to accept the situation as historical fact and move on in a healthier way by learning from the experience.

Sometimes we refuse to forgive because of what we consider justice. We think justice is supposed to be obvious (clear so we can see it), and directly connected to the previous event. That's how our man-made justice system works, so that's how we expect it to work

179

in the Universe. It doesn't. Everything man-made is flawed, the Universe is not. Universal justice is more along the lines of Newton's third law which states: "For every action, there is an equal and opposite reaction."

It's important to understand that no one gets away with anything, ever. No one can treat others poorly and feel good about themselves. Of course there are delusional people that think they can and say they can, but deep inside they are suffering. The levels of peace, happiness, and joy that open, loving people experience simply aren't accessible to someone that is closed off enough to hurt others. We are all connected in a spiritual sense; we are all one. As you understand that, you understand that if you hurt someone else, you're simply hurting yourself. There is literally no benefit to it. It's like getting mad at your finger and breaking it to get even—you just hurt yourself because it's part of you.

Sometimes appearances can be deceiving, welcome to spirituality. If you expect to live happily you will at some point need to live by faith, not by sight. I learned this in an extreme situation where it looked as though someone else was acting in a negative way and "winning" while I was acting in a loving way and "losing." I realized I needed to make peace with this somehow because it was robbing me of my joy. I remembered back to my dysfunctional days of making bad choices and hurting myself and others along the way—was I happy? NO! I was miserable. Even when I was completely self-absorbed and had stuffed all the feelings of inadequacy that were causing my dysfunction, I would still battle bouts of depression that I couldn't stave off.

There is no hiding from yourself. Everywhere you go, there you are. We know the things we've done; we can feel the energy vibration they carry. As long as we're living in detrimental ways towards others, we are being detrimental to ourselves because we are all one. So I had a choice. Do I begin to act in a negative way to try to "win" on the surface level while paying the price on the spiritual level through immense internal suffering? Or do I remain acting in a positive way understanding that *any* person acting in a negative way must be feeling the pain I felt before I woke up? The decision was easy, I would *never* go back to feeling the way I felt before I woke up, I wouldn't wish that on my worst enemy (if I had one).

This is when I truly understood that no one gets away with anything, even if it looks like it on the surface.

Forgiveness became much easier for me after that. It was clear that walking around with anger inside is the toxin that causes so much self-pain. It's been described as drinking poison and expecting the other person to die or picking up a hot coal intending to throw it at someone else. All you do is end up hurting yourself.

You cannot cause other people harm or "teach them a lesson" by being angry. The anger is inside of *you*. You are feeling the effects, not them. If they are going to feel bad about what they did, it's because of how they look at it, not because of how you look at it. So cut yourself a break, forgive someone for something they did, and pay attention to how you feel inside. If you've done it correctly, by accepting it and learning from it, you'll feel relief and peace where there used to be anger. If someone wronged you, why should you carry the painful feeling? You should carry peace inside. After all, you weren't the one who did something wrong! Forgive, free yourself, and get back to enjoying the good person you are.

Chapter 55

Who Are We to Judge?

Have you ever stopped to think about our ability to judge things? Of course, everyone feels they're making sound judgments most of the time, but what information are we using to make these judgments and do these judgments benefit us?

In most cases, we simply don't have the perspective or the information to make sound decisions on whether something is good or bad. Generally, we look at things very short term and do not consider the long-term effects. How can we? We can't see that far ahead. Take the example of Robert Jarvik, the inventor of the first permanently implantable artificial heart. When his father became ill with heart disease and had to have open-heart surgery, Jarvik became interested in medicine and began to think about possible designs for an artificial heart to help people like his father. I'm sure everyone thought it was a horrible thing that this boy's father had heart issues. Yet, understanding the severity of heart disease and the mortality of his father was the motivation that drove him to create the artificial heart, positively affecting millions of lives.

As it often happens, it took many years to be able to draw a straight line from cause to effect in this case. Since this is usually the way things happen, we'll get a broader understanding in another way. We can see that most change occurs through pain. When people experience enough discomfort, they change things. We can see this with addictions, with policy changes, with bad relationships, etc. It simply depends on the way we look at things to determine if they are good or bad. If an addict loses their job, it's bad. But if it gets them into recovery and they begin a healthy lifestyle and become a benefit to society, then it's good. If a place of business is treating their employees disrespectfully, it's bad. If people refuse to be treated that way and use it to learn self-worth and self-respect by setting better boundaries or finding a better job, that's good. You get the point, usually there's pain that induces change.

Some people will take horrible situations and argue the point. The fact is, we simply don't know. We don't know how negative things can develop healthy results. And if we don't know, who are we to judge? Prejudice is defined as an unfavorable opinion or feeling formed beforehand or without knowledge, thought, or reason. Most times, we don't have the information or long-term vision to make an informed judgment. I use the word prejudice because it has such a negative connotation and drives home the point that it should not be done. If we're simply thinking: "I'll try not to do that in the future"—you'll find yourself doing it. This is a deeply conditioned way of being that takes conscious attention and effort to change.

Lastly, what's the benefit of judging everything constantly? There isn't any. It encompasses us with negativity in such a way that we become hopeless. It's also bleeds into our daily lives with us judging other people, other cultures, other countries, and many other things that we simply don't have the proper information about. The worst side effect is that we begin to judge and punish ourselves endlessly for every decision we make that didn't turn out the way we wanted. We do this even though we didn't know any better at the time of the decision.

There's something very interesting about judgement—you either judge or you don't. You can't separate judging others and judging yourself; if you do one, you do the other. I learned this in an exercise I developed called "non-judgmental driving." I was having some stress issues while driving (a nice way of saying I was getting pissed off while driving) so I decided to address them. I decided to pause for a moment before starting the car and declare that this was going to be a non-judgmental drive. No matter what happened, no matter how obvious it was, I would not allow myself to judge anyone for anything while driving during this time. I did not have all the information necessary to make a fair assessment of someone else's driving, therefore I was not allowed to judge. I'm happy to report my driving experiences became much more enjoyable over the coming weeks.

The side effect that I didn't expect was that I found myself much happier in my personal life. I was feeling more joyful and took a brief inventory to find out why (I love learning from success). What have I done different lately? The only thing I could think of was the non-judgmental driving. That's when it occurred to me—the reason I'm happier is because I'm being kinder to myself, I'm judging myself less. I'm letting mistakes go without beating myself up and simply learning from them to enhance my life moving forward. I hadn't attempted to do this, it just happened. That's when I understood that judgement can't be separated; we either do it or we don't. If we don't judge, we experience much more happiness on a collective level as well as a personal level.

It's still beneficial to look at your mistakes and learn from the past. But letting go of the self-judgment, forgiving yourself, and doing better next time is much more productive than judging. When you know better, you do better.

Since I'm talking about driving, I'll offer you one more exercise that can help. I've done this myself with great success. The theory is that if we're going to judge, we have to judge fairly—good and bad. If I'm to judge people for driving poorly, I have to judge people for driving well. So I look at every car and notice how they're driving. I don't study every move they make looking for something negative, I simply look around. Occasionally I'll see someone doing something that isn't technically "correct." But within about sixty seconds I notice that 99% of the cars around me are driving fine. After about 30 cars, my brain usually gets the point. Almost everyone around me is driving fine. If one person irritates me during a 15 minutes drive, there were probably 500 cars near me that were driving fine. If I get irritated while driving, it's obviously not an accurate assessment, it's simply me being focused on the negative.

As you can see there is no good reason to judge, you're basically incapable of judging fairly because you don't have all the information necessary and you don't have the perspective to see how it plays out in the long-term. Judgement robs you of your joy and happiness because as you're judging others, you're judging yourself. Judgement also doesn't prevent you from making

185

mistakes in the future. Learning from your experiences does that. Judgement not only doesn't help but actually hinders your learning. I'm thinking this one's pretty clear at this point—if you'd like to be happy, stop judging everything and everyone including yourself.

Chapter 56

How to Stay Motivated in Your Spiritual Walk

Most people can get motivated, but how do we stay motivated when we don't feel like it? The answer is simple as all truth is, but it's not always easy.

Early in my spiritual life, I experienced an amazing sense of peace and contentment that I never wanted to lose. When I felt it slipping away at times, I did whatever was necessary to get it back. I learned to monitor my thoughts and feelings. When I noticed unhappiness surfacing, I did whatever it took to get back to my center and feel the peace and ease of life again.

Over the years, there were times when I got lazy and allowed myself to fall into negative thinking or moods. It felt easier than to put in the work to stay happy, but then I had to dig myself back out from way back where I let myself fall. I learned that if I put in some extra effort as soon as I noticed I was getting off track, I got back on track a lot faster. The longer I let myself drift, the longer the trek back to happiness was.

Now, when I notice myself falling off track, even if I don't "feel like it," I make the push. The motivation is simple: No matter how hard and how much effort it takes to get me back on track now, there's only one thing I know for sure. If I wait, it will be harder and take more effort. So I'll do what I have to do now.

Staying motivated is understanding that as soon as you notice something needs to be done for your betterment, peace, or happiness, do it right away. It's an easier and softer way to live, and you deserve to live the easier, softer way. I'm sure you've struggled enough for this lifetime!

Chapter 57

Living in the Flow

There is a flow to life. We've all felt it at one point or another. You know when everything just seems to be going right and it feels good. Even when something goes differently than we expected, we're able to shrug it off as inconsequential. Oh, it's wonderful when we're in it!

There are also times when we're not in the flow and everything is a struggle. Nothing seems to be going right, we break a shoelace and lose our mind! It happens. So, what's the difference?

I had a visual many years ago that's helped me tremendously. I was standing in a river trying to hold back the rushing water with two trash can lids. It was quite a struggle and as you can imagine, not working well at all. While I was standing there exhausted and frustrated, I had a thought: What if I stopped struggling against it and just surrendered and went with it? Exhausted as I was, I simply leaned backwards and allowed my feet to float up to the surface as my body began to float down the river. While I floated, I experienced twists and turns, excitement, fleeting moments of fear, happiness, peacefulness, sadness, joy, a feeling of love, laughter, etc. This ride had everything, except the struggle.

If we look closely at what's happening when we're in the flow of life, we'll notice that it's an alignment that's taking place. We are aligned with life's flow. We are going with life, instead of struggling against it. This doesn't mean it will be free of fear, sadness, or other difficult times. It means it will be free of struggle.

We are capable of handling difficult times, but what really hurts us is struggling against them. When something inside tells us that we

189

shouldn't be feeling this, it's not right, or it's not fair, this victim mentality zaps away our power. So, empower yourself to go with the flow, knowing that there is a higher purpose that's making things happen that we can't possibly understand fully.

This brief physical life is supposed to be filled with experiences, not safety. We can feel safety from our spiritual connection to the Eternal, the Universe, God, Creator, or Higher Power, etc. While we're here on earth, our lives will consist of many experiences. If we let go and go with the flow, it will be an amazing and wonderful ride. If we struggle against what's happening the whole way through, we'll suffer.

Chapter 58

Growing into Your New Way of Being

The fact that we're human beings with a physical body vibrating at a certain rate is helpful in understanding the growth process. In terms of shifting and raising our vibration, there are two main ways on opposite ends of the spectrum with a lot of gray area in between. On one end, you have spontaneous, overwhelming spiritual awakenings and on the other end, you have a progressive, learned style of awakening. Most people fall somewhere in the middle and experience a series of both: an occasional, large realization followed by many small insights on a daily, weekly, or monthly basis.

In the learned style, growth begins with a small insight, a shift of perspective. This can happen in various ways, including contemplation and meditation, through a conversation, or being exposed to a teaching. This shift of perspective is mostly mental, rooted in the intellect; although it can have some smaller vibrational body components. Of course, this initial insight is a wonderful beginning. However, it's important to know that we need to thoroughly shift our body vibration when we're going through a transformative process.

Divine Knowledge knows this, and Life gives us an opportunity to live what we have learned. Once we stand in our new Truth, our new perspective, our new way of Being, and interact with life in this manner, our whole body vibration shifts. It is said that no Faith is true until it's tried. We need to act in the manner that expresses who we are becoming in a real life situation before we can fully become the change we are going through.

Often, we learn something intellectually and think we're all set. We've transcended it and it's no longer an issue in our lives. Soon, a situation arises that challenges what we learned and suddenly we think we must have failed and never learned what we thought we did. We assume the situation is arising because we're not where we're supposed to be, that we did something wrong, or brought it on by living in a negative way. When a challenging situation we're trying to transcend shows up in our lives, it's there so we can transcend it, not because we did something wrong. It's an opportunity—not a punishment or a test.

Here's an example for clarity. After a conversation with a teacher, you gain insight on how your family triggers an insecurity and why it happens. In this moment, you experience a shift of perspective that's exciting. You're relieved that you understand and you no longer need to live the way you've been living since you now have clarity about the whole situation. This is great; however, it's only intellectual.

Soon, Life will present an opportunity to stand in this new clarity so that you can raise your vibration and transcend this issue permanently. When you begin to get triggered, you have a choice. You can fall back into the old way of Being, the way of the victim, or you can catch it and lean into your new way of Being.

The point is you really need to stand in it and choose to behave differently, based on the new way of processing the information around your family trigger. When you are aware of this process, you can keep your eyes open and be ready for the situation to arise. Now you're much more prepared to catch it and stand in your new way of Being. When left unaware, that old way of Being has a strong pull and an intoxicating familiarity that can suck you in before you know it.

So, know the process and understand that once you learn something, life will soon give you an opportunity to embody it. Only after you stand in it, Be it, and embody it, does it become part of you. This is what shifts your vibration physically to create a new, healthier vibrational Being. Now, you vibrate at the higher rate of someone who handles those situations with grace and ease.

Occasionally, if it's a big shift, you may have to stand in your new Truth a few times to really anchor into it. Or, if Life sees you falling back into an old way of Being, it can give you an opportunity to stand in it as a reminder before you fall back completely.

This isn't a big deal. Once you're able to stand in your new Truth, it's not as difficult as it used to be and it doesn't feel like you're being subjected to torturous testing. It's simply a reinforcement of what you're already capable of doing. If you're being mindful, it's not only a non-issue but it's fun and empowering to stand unphased in something that used to bother you. Being able to see and stand in the change you wanted to happen is a joyful and opening experience all in itself!

Chapter 59

Be Who You Are Becoming

Often times, people work very hard on themselves to become happier, more successful, more grounded, more connected, more peaceful, etc. This is a wonderful undertaking. Unfortunately, they often get caught up in the "doing" and never get to the "Being."

The world we live in is very linear. It progresses from one stage to another sequentially. Think of school. We learn certain things sequentially until someone tells us we passed the class, or we graduated. Then, we know we're done. With self-growth, it's not linear. There is no graduation, no ending. It's just a journey picking up pieces of Truth along the way and constantly becoming a better version of ourselves. So, when do we get to experience the fruits of our labor? When do we get to live in the joyful existence we've worked so hard to create?

The answer is *now!* If you're caught up seeking, you'll never find. The truth is that your happiness is here...right now. You can take in much self-knowledge and many new perspectives, but the time to implement them and feel the joy of experiencing them is now. So make sure to be happy, peaceful, and feel these things as you walk your walk. "Be" the person you've worked so hard to become. You've done the work, so go reap the rewards.

One of the best ways to do this is to take a giant step back from your current life and put it into perspective. Who were you 10 years ago? Five years ago? Last year? What have you learned in the last six months? How have you changed? If you've been working on yourself, the changes can be dramatic. If they're not, perhaps you should seek some help or assess what you've done that's worked

195

and what you've done that didn't work. If you haven't been working on yourself, start now. Otherwise, the future is going to look like the present. If you don't change—nothing changes. Your external life is a reflection of your internal life.

You don't have to "finish" to experience happiness, there is no "key" to happiness. Happiness is a decision, it does not depend on your circumstances. You can have it today...now. Learning can be one of the most addictive things out there. What happens is, we read a book or listen to an audio recording and because of the positivity and energy of it, we feel better. There's a newfound sense of hope pumping through us and it feels good because our suffering has subsided a little. Unconsciously we mistake this for actual change. We get addicted to the cycle. Get some spiritual food, feel better; take in some positivity, feel better. If we're feeling down, we take in some positivity, then we're not feeling so down. The way you can tell this is not sustainable is that your source of positivity and happiness is coming from outside yourself. Happiness only comes from within, it cannot be based on something in the external, constantly changing world if it is to be counted on.

Be happy during your journey; don't wait, expecting it to surface once you've learned enough or read the right book. It's already inside you waiting to be accessed. So simply access it and then continue growing in the energy of happiness.

For many of you reading this, you may not be giving yourself the credit you deserve. If you've applied energy towards your own growth consistently, you've probably come farther than you realize. Remember, there is no finish line. The time to enjoy life and your newfound outlook is now. Life happens when you're busy doing other things, including spiritual things and self-help things. Don't get so busy learning and growing that you miss the opportunity to experience the joy of living. Your life is now...enjoy it now!

Chapter 60

Spiritual Maturity

There comes a time in our spiritual lives where we need to trust what we've learned, what we've become, and the way the Universe works. Of course, it's helpful to continually gather new information, hear things again in new ways, and review the lessons learned. Remember that within us, we have everything we need to move forward, to live peacefully, happily, and in alignment with All that is. After a while, it's necessary to lean on what we've learned and trust it.

One of the best ways to do this is to stop trying to figure out everything. Is this person right for me relationship-wise? Is this the right job? Should I move? Should I get divorced? These big questions will be answered in time. But usually, we want to know *now*, before we have enough information. In my experience, if you keep working on you and continue being present, happy, connected, and joyful, all these things will work out. The answers bubble up to the surface effortlessly when we stop trying to control the outcome of things before their time.

What we need to do is to continue gathering information. Instead of trying to figure things out, just trust that you'll see the answer when it appears...because you will! If you're not sure about something, you simply don't have enough information. If you're not sure about someone, go on a couple more dates. It will become glaringly obvious if you should or should not be with them. Look around for other jobs and compare what you have with what's out there. If you are meant to change jobs, the ideal one will appear. You will recognize it if your heart is open, if you've done the work, if you're happy and focused on living a life filled with love and joy. Don't worry, you're not going to miss it!

Disclaimer: What I'm talking about next is garden variety dysfunctional relationships that breed frustration, not physical violence. If you or someone else is in physical danger, it's a different situation. Most likely, you will need to create a plan to make sure you're safe first and get out as soon as possible.

In a difficult marriage, if you stop worrying about what's wrong with the other person and just keep working on yourself, it will become obvious if it will work out or it won't. In this situation, we often think we know it won't work out when we really have no idea. It's just frustration talking. The difference is in the energy of how you're saying it.

The way of frustration is when you find yourself saying things like: "They're never going to change." "I can't take this anymore." "There's no use trying." "They're not interested in trying." Usually, things are more focused on the other person or the other person's behavior, and you feel frustration inside.

The other way is out of self-love and calmness. Now, don't try to fool yourself into getting here. If you say you're acting out of self-love but you still feel like you can't take it anymore, that's not self-love. You will yell things like "I don't deserve this" and "I'm leaving because I love myself!" This is not self-love. Self-love is calm, effortless, and easy. Self-love doesn't have a ton of emotion or drama. It's more matter of fact. It's obvious and kind. Look for that. Work on yourself until you feel that. When you can tell yourself calmly and peacefully that it's time to move on, that the relationship isn't good for either one of you and it feels like love talking, then you're probably there. Compare it to when you were feeling frustrated. Is it different? *Really* different? If so, you're good.

If you're considering a move, a career change, a new hobby, etc., gather information and pay attention to how you feel until the answer arises. This is a skill you can develop. You need to have the maturity to lean back and trust that you'll see the answer when it arises. Trust yourself and the Universe to co-exist and co-create the future that will bring you the most joy. This is dealing with life in a spiritually mature way.

Do the work and trust the work that you've done. Be who you hoped to be. Act how you wanted to act. Relax and trust in the way that will bring peace to your everyday life. You are cared for, loved, and the whole Universe is conspiring in your favor. Trust it, trust yourself, and say, "Thank you."

Chapter 61

Why a Better You Means a Better World

When looking at the state of affairs in the world, many people are wondering what we can do to change things. To answer this, consider what Gandhi meant when he said, "Be the change you wish to see in the world." This phrase means more than just working on ourselves for our own benefit, although there are certainly great rewards at this level alone.

If you take this statement deeper to an energetic level, you can understand how collective change occurs. Each of us has our own energy field, which is connected to the collective energy field. These fields have vibrational rates. As we work on ourselves and raise the vibration of our personal energy fields to a higher, healthier level, the vibration of the collective energy field that we're connected to also rises. This develops an atmosphere more conducive to change.

The lighter an energy field, the easier it is for people to change. When someone is stuck in an old, negative way of Being, the energy is dense with a low vibration. When they are surrounded by an atmosphere of lightness, it's easier for them to let go of old ways of Being and open up to new, lighter, healthier ways of Being. So, as we change our own personal vibrational rate, we experience more joy in our lives and contribute to a collective atmosphere that's friendlier to change.

Not only is the atmosphere more conducive to change but it's lighter, it feels better, and there's literally more love in the air. There is less dysfunction, less crime, less hate, and less lack. We are creating a new heaven and a new earth, as they say, little by little through each awakening soul. The tipping point is 51 percent. All we have to do is get to the point where there's more people focused on being happy than on being right and the tides will turn dramatically in our favor.

I'm going to close out with a quote from Jimi Hendrix:

> "When the power of love overcomes the love of power the world will know peace."

Go inside, do the work, shine brightly, and know that by Being a better You, you're creating a better world.

About the Author

Glenn Ambrose

Glenn Ambrose is a Spiritual Teacher, Life Coach, Speaker, and the Host of the popular podcast *Life, Lessons, & Laughter with Glenn Ambrose*. He is an internationally certified Life Coach through the Fowler Wainwright International Institute of Professional Coaching and has been working with clients all over the world for many years. In 2003, homeless, addicted to alcohol, and on death's doorstep, Glenn's life took a 180° turn. Through a series of powerful Spiritual Awakenings, he gained a fundamental understanding of Spiritual Law which he teaches in a practical, down to earth way, helping countless others with these foundational insights. Glenn was born and raised in Massachusetts, he enjoyed 14 years raising his son Matteo in Rhode Island, and now they live in Florida, the tropical setting that he so enjoys!

Glenn's philosophy is that happiness and fulfillment are there for everyone to have, and are attainable by anyone. Combining his coaching skills with his finely tuned style for getting to the heart of the matter, he inspires the change that is necessary for truly successful living. After finding happiness himself, he immediately saw that it is accessible for anyone as long as they have the willingness to open up to it. His specialty is taking people who are open to growth, helping them recognize what their individual challenges are to finding the fulfillment they desire, and then strategizing small, simple steps to follow in order for them to reach that fulfillment.

Glenn is well-known for his passion, enthusiasm, and ability to see things from a clear perspective which gives him the aptitude to guide people to an effective path for their own self-discovery and happiness. He uplifts others to come out of their complacency or struggle and experience the levels of contentment and joy that are possible.

> "There is nothing more powerful and heart-warming to me than to see that sparkle in someone's eye or hear the elation in their voice when they get that first spark of pure hope, and it hits deep inside of them, that not only is happiness possible but it's right there for them to grasp!"
> ~ Glenn Ambrose

You can find Glenn and access his podcasts, blogs and services at his website: GlennAmbrose.com